Robert L. Peck

Personal Development Center
Lebanon, Connecticut
U.S.A. 2001
www.personaldevcenter.com

3 4 5 6 7 8 9 10

Publisher's Note

This is a third printing, January 2022, of the original 2001 publication of Finding Power by Robert L. Peck. It contains minor editorial corrections throughout the text as well as format improvements of the Ancient Individual Control System in the Appendix.

Personal Development Center
P.O. Box 93
South Windham, CT 06266-0093

ISBN 10 Paperback: 0-917828-08-9
ISBN 13 Paperback: 978-0-917828-08-9

ISBN 10 e-book: 0-917828-13-5
ISBN 13 e-book: 978-0-917828-13-3

Cover design by: Lois Rivard

Printed in the United States of America

Table of Contents

Appendix

PREFACE

This book is about the mental and physical powers that lie behind Greatness. They can be seen in the passerby who does the miraculous and saves some child from death, in the inventor who solves some need of society, in the leader who guides a nation or group into a new world, or in the individuals who solve their problems using unexpected sudden insights and strengths. An explanation of these powers is based upon:

1. The conversion of energy into different forms,
2. A coupling with the future, and
3. The usage of an efficient but little-known energy-mental-physical control system within the body.

Those individuals who perform great deeds requiring special powers generally credit their powers to following a basic dedication to accomplish some task with an unshakable faith in their future. On a personal level this can be restated as, whatever you are truly dedicated to in life can be found. This book describes how your expectation of the future can mystically shape your present world. Stated another way, by reaching for or creating something in the future, the present is changed to allow the attainment of what is desired. This is, however, in direct contradiction with the strong social teaching that you must concentrate upon the immediate moment and try harder. Yet trying, as almost everyone knows, only results in things getting worse.

This book is also a primer in creating change in your life and gives you the essentials that self-help books leave out, namely the "how to." It is apparent that few people understand what is required to change or what change is. The general assumption is that it is something that is acquired, absorbed, or just happens by believing or some other mysterious process. Changing is actually a precise, well-understood process that has been fully explored in engineering circles. This highly developed science will be simply explained in this book and can then be applied to changing your life using some practical yet esoteric and forgotten models of the body and mind.

The author, a scientist and teacher, draws heavily from the experiences of his students as well as from ancient writings and his professional experience with energy conversion and process control. He starts with explaining the supernormal and supernatural powers in terms that are both acceptable to modern science and also verifiable with your own individual experience. He leads the reader into looking at common everyday experiences like controlling the throwing of a ball and then describes in simple terms the inner operation of the body and mind. He also gives the description of the creative process and its dependency upon a special energy in the body as well as a connection with the future.

finding POWER

CHAPTER ONE
SUPER POWERS

One essential effort of a stable institution is that it must suppress and hide the existence of superpowers in its members. Because of these efforts, almost all of the members in a society perceive the power of an institution as being far greater than their own. One of the old, well-known maxims of the ruling classes is that the masses must not be allowed to find the powers that reside within them. Only the ruling elect or the institution must be perceived to hold the controlling power. The masses must be taught that they are weak, helpless and must obey. Only when this occurs can the masses be taught to become civilized and follow societal law.

The world's great religious teachers agreed that the masses first must master and be subject to the laws of society. However, once they had mastered social interactions then they might find the existence of a superpower deep within themselves and use that inner power to further transform and change their entire world. The early religious teachings explained how you could find freedom from the limiting and false teachings of institutions and find self-determinacy. Institutions, in seeking power over the masses, subverted these teachings of an inner individual superpower by stating that:

1. The teachers were saying that the power was contained in an institution and the *you* was a collective you and did not mean you as an individual.
2. Since they had the power and not you as an individual, they could interpret what the original teachings meant.
3. They or the collective you, as an institution, were able to overcome and protect you from those other *false* institutions.

4. You must bow and be subject to the power of the institution.[1]

Modern science, which has declared itself outside of the religious debates, has nonetheless contributed to the concept that you do not have an inner power and that you should be subject to institutions. Modern materialistic science negates creditable knowledge coming forth solely from inspired religious leaders as well as the existence of any inner superpower within individuals. In comparison with the religious statements above, science promotes the following questionable teachings:

1. Only science can write or define absolute law.
2. Any power or energy must be tangible and therefore described by the written laws of science.
3. The authority of science cannot be questioned, since the power of science is believed to be approaching that of the god of religions and some assert that it may someday even create life.
4. Science is an institution and an accredited arm of academia (and government).[2]

This modern stance of science is, however, very much at odds with the beginning of science that began with the recognition of three supernatural and non-tangible powers called Law, Energy and Life (as described later). These three powers comprise the creative and sustaining force of all that exists or will ever exist.

Despite the efforts of science and religion, some individuals do rise above the limitations and false beliefs imposed by society and discover that they can, in fact, become whatever they really dedicate themselves to. They can do the nearly impossible in times of crisis. They can create new approaches, methods and

[1] See Book 2, Chapters 11-13.
[2] Ibid.

solutions to problems. They can lead others into new worlds. They are even capable of finding the mythical ecstasy of life. Since these individuals are instrumental in making a better society, neither science nor religion can directly or forcibly oppose them if society is to advance. Historically, however, the creative individuals remain at the fringes of social acceptability without direct support.

Before they become fully developed and controlled by institutions, children are obvious examples of the existence of some fundamental superpowers that almost everyone can perceive. It is the manifesting of the inner powers of childhood that enables children to rise above the animal world and to start to become civilized and subject to institutions. To more fully appreciate this miracle of childhood, consider studying children other than your own, such as observing a foreign child able to speak Russian or Greek within a year. Children learning to do abstract reasoning and create wild imaginary games further points to some deep inner creative power. Each family can be seen as producing children with the family's language, beliefs, life styles, expressions and thinking within an incredibly short period of time.

The pursuit of an inner power can therefore begin with the question, why is it that you as an adult cannot change yourself with many months of effort while a child can quickly obtain an even greater change in a matter of days?

You may well answer this question with the assertion that children must have a special energy or power that you have lost over the years. Then another question is, how can some exceptional adults find an energy to do even greater feats than children such as changing themselves, their world, and those around them? It seems obvious that if you wish to change yourself and your world, you will require some of this special energy that you once had as a child. With this revived fundamental power, you will also require additional power that is directed toward some specific task, as will be discussed.

This book will identify the energy and power to change as being supernormal forces that arise from supernatural sources. The meanings of supernatural and supernormal powers have been vastly distorted over the recent years with the modern view that neither of these powers actually exists. The modern world in its attachment to everything being materialistic and everyone being equal must deny these hidden and special powers. Charlatans who falsely claim to be able to violate the laws of physics or nature are also contributing to the disbelief in supernatural powers. Science is perhaps the greatest source of doubt in the supernatural, since Science attempts (falsely) to state that Science does not include the supernatural. Despite this overt denial, this chapter will continue to prove that supernatural and supernormal forces do, in fact, exist and are supportable by science and personal experience.

First consider the term *supernormal*. *Super* means "above" and supernormal is defined as any action that is above the normal. Statistics demonstrates that any physical trait can be characterized by a *normal* distribution curve that gives the numbers of people possessing a particular magnitude of that trait. Such a statistical curve can be consulted to find, for instance, what percentage of people can throw a rock a particular distance. The average distance that a rock can be thrown is then easily found by finding what distance has the most numbers of people associated with it. Some people throw farther than this and some throw less. As you count people throwing farther and farther from the average, the numbers of people decrease until perhaps only one can throw a particular rock 1,000 feet and only one cannot throw the rock any further than three feet. The people who throw the rock the farthest are therefore supernormal or very far above the normal while the three-foot throw is subnormal. Modern statistics tends to define average characteristics as being those held by 70% of the population with 15% above and below the average. The level of being supernormal would constitute the upper level of the above average. Early religions generally pushed the limit for super-normality to one in a thousand or even one in ten thousand[3] or that those who mastered or manifested the religious teachings were very peculiar or special people. The important criterion about being supernormal is that it can be expected and, although rare, is attainable, such as with practice or demand.

Super*natural* powers, on the other hand, are above the supernormal powers and have a source that cannot be measured by any known methods. Consider the two supernatural forces of Life and Energy. Only when they become manifest can they be evidenced. Life and Energy are abstract and cannot be perceived in their natural or non-manifested state. Neither Energy nor Life can be created or isolated in any laboratory. Life and Energy cannot be described other than by pointing to their results.

This book will add one more criterion to the description of supernatural powers and that is that once they are manifested, they cannot have violated any law of nature. In other words, something is not created out of nothing and the appearance of the product of the supernatural power must be fully explained and fit fully into the current world. This definition eliminates such things as levitation, instant cures, or production of gold or objects from the air. It does include, however, the limited changing of your future, union with other minds and actions, and creating such things as new concepts, machines, designs, health, expressions and social interactions.

Supernatural power sources must lie outside of the normal physical world yet are capable of changing the physical world in such a way that the results can be measured. There is no way, for instance, of telling how much energy is in a can of some

[3] Ecclesiastes 7:28; Gospel of Thomas, verse 23

fluid nor of measuring how much creativity some person is capable of, other than by measuring how well the fluid burns or evaluating the produced creations of that person. Supernatural powers lie outside of the awareness of the physical world, yet the results of the manifesting power physically change the world and can be measured. Supernatural powers are potential powers only and when manifested belong to the physical world.

Perhaps the original concept of supernatural power can be understood by looking back into the ancient world when the cause of rain and the budding of new leaves in spring was not known. To the ancients, the cause was supernatural since they had no way of observing, measuring or studying these primal powers. The effects of these supernatural powers were, however, very real and manifest. One typical method of controlling these powers was to assign a supernatural god with controlling powers living in a supernatural place. The barrier between the real world and the supernatural world could then be bridged with the beginning of religion with its worship and ritual.

In attempting to distance itself from any religion or priesthood, Science denied the god concept and at the same time threw out any consideration for the non-explainable or non-measurable. Science was to be concerned only with physical reality. Science has, however, steadily explained the various powers that the ancients called supernatural powers of the gods. At the present time it may be considered that there are only three basic supernatural powers left unexplained which are Energy, Life, and Law. (Law will be equated to creation and creativity later,[4] but for the moment can be considered to be the law of nature.)

Physics is still worshiping a god called Energy with many scientists believing that they write Law. Biology likewise has made no inroads on defining the god of Life or the life force. None of

[4] See Chapters 11 and 12.

the sciences know the source or even the full manifesting of these three powers, where they stay nor what they are, or how to measure them. These three powers are supernatural, mystical, and spiritual.[5] They are certainly not physical elements. Energy, for instance, is very strange in that it can take many different forms from being heat and light, to motion, sound and electricity. No one knows what *pure* Energy looks like or how to measure it. It can only be tabulated when it changes its form as, for instance, from a chemical form in a can of gasoline into fire.

Similarly, what is the Life force? It, too, is only evidenced when it manifests into some physical form. Life force is hidden and only evidenced with new growth. Science observes how a plant will reach for and change its own future as it pushes forth new growth to reach for sunlight yet science cannot explain or measure the power behind this amazing and supernatural power to change the future. Similarly, humans use the Life force to change their own future as they reach for new worlds. You cannot, however, point to any one plant or individual and state how, what and when it will change in the future.

There is a sense of reverence about the word Law that points to a supernatural power that is non-manifested, mysterious and mystical. Modern interpretation of Law is generally applied to something that is written that states what is or what should be. To Religion, Law was given to certain prophets who wrote it all down, and to Science, it was written by researchers who wrestled the truth from nature. Both Religion and Science worship the written law and hold it as inviolate. To both, access to the source of law is only gained within the sacred halls of academia or the priesthood and any pronouncements upon it must be approved by the governing institution. Law is therefore generally not supernatural but rather the institutionally approved physical writings of individuals.

---

[5] Ibid.

Supernatural Law is, however, something that directs what is and what will happen and is not a mere description of what does or did happen. Law is the source of the written laws and is behind everything that is in physical existence, as will be elaborated upon in Chapter Eleven.

Creativity is almost synonymous with Law in that it is also supernatural and can become the source of new Law. Religion gives an accurate and logical description of this relationship in such statements that a god created Law. Science has no explanation as to the source of either Law, Energy or Life, yet has demonstrated that science is capable of creating new Law through its physical and mental creations that change the entire world, as for example, the birth control pill and the transistor. Science in this sense is acting as did the ancient God of the Bible. Similarly, some individuals can so alter their lives that there can be no question, that somehow they changed the original Law governing their life. This change must be equated with some inner creative and miraculous power. As will be discussed later, you can bring the intangible and unseen creative power into your daily life such that you are able to go beyond your limited training and skills and produce the unexpected.

The next important consideration is the source of Law. To religions, the source of Law or the governing rules of the universe is from the power of God or from Creation. Scientists seldom discuss the source of Law, but if they were to attempt to do so, they would probably define it as do the religions as coming forth from some creative force. In both cases, creation is something that took place in the dim past before the existence of anything.

Creativity is, however, still manifest in the modern world as new concepts, devices and viewpoints come forth from some hidden source. This coming forth from some inner hidden source has been called *knowing*. The word knowing has lost much of its original meaning with the modern rejection of supernatural and supernormal powers. Knowing has erroneously come to mean the same as having wisdom in the same manner as does a computer or an encyclopedia. The word knowing was derived from the same root as *gnosis* in Greek or *jnana* in Sanskrit that means to comprehend something in suddenness and completeness without learning. With this definition *knowing* is the same as expressing Truth.

The supernatural aspect of knowing has suffered a long history of suppression. The early religious sects, such as the Gnostics, who practiced supernatural knowing or *gnosis*, were persecuted and killed as possessing powers or Truth that only government or religion should possess. Any government or institution must claim to have more power and knowledge than its members. Kingdoms in the past, for example, were ruled by kings who had the "Divine Right of Kings" and because of this right could not be questioned nor could anyone else claim to have this right.

There is another form of the supernatural that is of main interest in this book and that is the power that can change future events. As an example, consider the old practice of *giving your word*. Word, in this case, implied a supernatural power that would control what would take place in the future. The person who gave their word could be trusted to produce what the word described. There is a phrase in the New Testament that is taken from the earlier Indian *Vedas* that states that in the beginning was the Word and that everything was made by the Word. This concept of Word or the description of what will be is still extant in the modern world. This is evidenced primarily in success stories, and is typified by some children from the ghetto who give their word to themselves or others that they will obtain some goal in life and then go on to achieve it. If asked about how they could make such a promise, they will generally specify that they knew and could see their own created future.

Changing, defining or creating the future certainly requires a unique type of energy to supply the power to make a change as will be discussed in Chapter Four, and the results are seldom instantaneous nor clearly perceived before they occur. The intention or dedication seems to be able to only give a direction to an outcome, but never specific results. The results are, however, spectacular and seemingly miraculous when observed over a long period of time. One conclusion as to the supernatural power of changing the future is that it is a weak power that requires a continuous exertion over a long period of time to become effective. Chapter Thirteen discusses this subject in greater detail and cites some interesting supportive scientific research.

Now back to supernormal powers. They are quite obvious and observable in comparison to supernatural powers. You know of people who demonstrate supernormal powers by standing well above their peers or by having a control over their life, family, work, recreation and religious experiences that those around them cannot find. Abraham Maslow (1993) called these people *self-actualized.* These people are those creative individuals who change their world and the people within their world. They improve the world with their lives and many leave an indelible mark long after their passage from the world.

In general, the supernormal is evidenced by exceptional people meeting some strong need. Meeting a strong need is, however, preceded by a strong commitment or dedication to improving life before they do the spectacular or supernormal. As an example, a person who suddenly dashes into an unfamiliar burning building and rescues a child in the flames and smoke has had to have a certain level of physical and mental capabilities as well as a strong dedication to others long before the rescue. These individuals can be described as knowing life and others in that they go beyond the normal social level of caring or doing their social duty and instead see the supernormal forces of life. Supernormal events do not happen to those who are not prepared, cannot see what is required, or are unwilling to work or to trust in their own developed future.

Supernormal occurrences do happen to those who expect the supernatural to guide them in their daily life and do not attempt to judge their every action. This is exemplified by a favorite verse[6] of the author that states that an individual can set the direction of their path through life, but supernatural forces or the Divine controls the steps.

[6] Proverbs 16:9 "A man's heart devises his way, but the Lord directs his steps."

CHAPTER TWO
CHANGING

The modern world is full of hucksters who sell change. You can purchase a weekend retreat that promises to change you into a loving person or into a dynamic entrepreneur. You can purchase a book that promises to change your religious doubts to religious fervor. You can buy a computer program that will supposedly turn your child into a superior student. Then, of course, there are those pills that you can get from your doctor that offer a wide variety of changes. Change is generally equated to a cost and is something obtained from an institution, but never equated to an inner process within yourself.

This book will describe the inner process of changing that requires a special inner energy coupled with a particular mental view of the future, none of which are taught, discussed or tolerated in many social circles. Interestingly, almost everyone has experienced the inner power of change and this book will work closely with your personal experiences to verify the statements in the book. We start, therefore, with the experienced magic of throwing or hitting a ball.

Everyone who attempts to learn how to hit or throw a ball learns that *follow through* is necessary to increase the control over where the ball will go. A few people who think about follow through cannot see any connection between what they do after the ball leaves their hands and where it goes. They may ask, "Why should it matter what my arms do once the ball leaves?" They are assured, however, that follow through is very important and that what the arms do after the ball leaves does somehow change the flight of the ball. Later experiences prove this to be true.

The mystery of the future effecting the throw is further compounded by the followers of the Zen-type schools who teach that it does not matter so much about the follow through, as long as you concentrate upon where the ball will end up. Somehow, concentrating upon the target of the ball affects how the ball is released. In other words, your vision of the future target changes the manner of releasing the ball so that it will indeed hit the spot that is concentrated upon. This sounds like pure magic! Consider, for instance, the stories of how the baseball hero, Babe Ruth would point to where the ball was going to go when he went up to bat, which it many times did.

The control of the ball can be extended even one step more by concentrating not on where the ball will go, but rather where it will do the most good. The expert tennis player concentrates not on hitting the ball, but rather upon the returned ball catching the opposing player off balance. This is similar to endowing the ball with a magic power that knows where it should go to be most effective. Athletes have a name for this experience and call it *stepping into the zone*. In the zone, a football quarterback knows that the ball will be caught by the intended receiver.

Great athletes and coaches know that the state of mind is critical in regard to physical performance. The majority of coaches and athletes will agree that immediate success is highly dependent upon the expectation of finding success in the future. If an athletic team expects to be beaten, chances are that it will be beaten. However, a winning team that expects to win has interactions between its players that are more orientated toward a future success than toward the play itself. For example, a quarterback and receiver can find that mystical space in time where they know that a pass will be completed. This expectation of success does indeed shape the future action on the field as well as shape the future successes in your life.[7]

This book is not concerned with the normal strategies for winning used by coaches and athletes, but rather concentrates upon

[7] See Chapter 12.

those rare supernatural occurrences that could not be planned beforehand or even expected. Under the stress and demand of intense competition the individual athlete can find a supernatural power that allows the future need to shape the immediate action. Under this power, the athlete knows what will happen and that knowledge shapes the athlete's present actions such that the future becomes real.

When the mind envisions the landing of the ball rather than upon the throwing or hitting, the brain no longer is consciously deciding how to position or control the body. Some argue that by taking the concentration off of the form of the body, the body can perform much better. This is based upon the experience of how conditioned thinking gets in the way of the body's motion. This is certainly true in many cases as will be discussed later, but there is an even more important aspect of this process.

Letting the future control the present actions becomes very mystical in that it requires the body of the athlete to respond not only to the envisioned landing of the ball, but also to whatever the future might become. Consider again the game of tennis or football, where the future motions of your opponent(s) are not clearly known. Under these conditions it is not enough to know where your ball will go, but also you must somehow know where others will be or how they will respond. This requires the ball not to go to a particular place (as envisioned), but rather that it will go where it will do the most good (based upon the actual future action). A tennis player may describe the situation later that he knew somehow that his opponent would be off balance as the ball left the racket. Many football athletes, for example, report that when they are in the zone time slows way down and their awareness extends to the whole playing field. In such a space the quarterback and receiver both know of the spot where the catch will be successful, although that spot was not initially known.

The following scenario gives one more related example of the future shaping the activities in the oncoming moment. A schoolteacher needs to teach a class about the power of political activity and has no immediate answer as to how this is going to be done, yet has the strong feeling that somehow when the time comes, the answer will be there. Next day, on the way out the door, this teacher grabs the evening paper to use for a drop cloth for some painting and still does not have a clue as to how the teaching assignment will be carried out. However, upon arriving in the classroom, she finally places the paper on the floor and then notices one of the articles that becomes the perfect example to use for the class.

Everyone knows people like this teacher who appear to *wing it* or wait for inspiration to come at the last minute and somehow, to the consternation of their fellow workers, do an even better job than they do with all of their worries and efforts. The observers, not understanding the actual effort in obtaining and maintaining a future expectation, see success as being only due to luck. Most original religious writings have a statement that success can be obtained when you have a strong dedication, faith, and vision of the future.

The future controlling your present activities can be further exemplified when you find yourself in one of your bad days when everything is going wrong and you wait essentially for the next bad thing to happen, and it generally does! You know that somehow you are projecting something into your own future that, in turn, is causing your own misery. You may attempt to describe it in terms of cause and effect as perhaps having gotten out of the wrong side of the bed, but if so, how can you change it? The process is in motion heading toward a dismal future; you are well aware of it, yet you feel powerless to change it. You may relate it to the thrown ball that is not going where you intended it to go, but how can you change it if it is already in motion? With the cause-and-effect model, you cannot, of course, change your destiny. Yet if it is a process, then your follow through or expectation of a successful future coupled with faith can and does indeed change your future.

BOOK ONE

CONTROL

CHAPTER THREE
CONTROL OR CHANGE

"Control yourself!" This is a common command and generally means to stop what you are doing. This concept of what controlling means is widespread in our modern world. Controlling of the self generally means to conform rather than to control. An individual is supposed to be controlled by the outside world rather than by the self. An individual is supposed to be controlled by the evening news and hence 'popular' opinion and not by individual studies or research. The control of the body is likewise governed by conditioning starting from early childhood or in repetitive learning processes. Most self-help books stress attaining more learned responses that are added to the unwanted responses rather than controlling or changing the unwanted responses. Individuals, in summary, are not taught about controlling themselves or even what control consists of.

In contrast to the lack of teachings about social and personal controls, the technical and highly productive commercial world is full of very effective and efficient controls consisting of interactive control systems. Many of these control systems are highly complex such as found in automated assembly lines or computer-controlled space ships. Engineering uses such controls to keep our buildings comfortable, our food clean and well-preserved, transportation safe and reliable, entertainment spectacular yet affordable, communication worldwide, and the supply chain of life's necessities unbroken. The business world is likewise well controlled with managers and administrators versed in how to optimize the interaction of individuals and equipment toward reaching some defined goal.

Surprisingly, the science of control that is used in controlling an automated assembly line can be applied to understanding and perfecting the inner control of an individual. Furthermore, the body and mind have controlling elements whose capabilities in many ways surpass those in the most advanced technical control systems. There are only six essential control elements used in the most elaborate control systems and these six elements are easy to find and use in controlling your world. These elements are, however, generally unknown or unused by psychologists and sociologists who generally believe that it is nearly impossible to significantly change after the age of eight or thereabouts. Another surprising aspect of the controlling elements within an individual is that these control elements were described in some ancient writings long before the development of psychology as will be discussed in the appendix.

The fundamental function of control systems is to turn on or off a source of power that effectuates some desired result. This requires the availability of a source of power that can supply the energy to power the change, the knowledge or data of what is desired, the knowledge of how well the power is doing, and then some manner of turning on or off or moderating the source of power. Control, whether of a machine or an individual, consists of six separate components:

1. the source of power for change,
2. an actuator or main power control and selector,
3. a sensor that measures what is being changed,
4. a comparator,
5. converters,
6. the data or description of what is desired.

The common thermostat for controlling room temperature can be used to illustrate all six of the above elements. The main function of the thermostat, as with most control systems, is to turn on or off a source of energy (1) to heaters that heat a room to some preset temperature. The switch that turns the energy on or off is called the actuator (2) normally mounted on a bimetallic strip that bends with temperature and serves as a sensor (3) as well as a comparator (4) to the preset temperature data (6) obtained by turning the bimetallic strip or switch. The converters (5) can be of several types ranging from hot water radiators, infrared emitters, electric heaters to hot air coming from a blower and furnace. The switch is generally provided with a further adjustment of the comparator (4) that sets the sensitivity of the thermostat or how much the temperature must drop before the thermostat activates the system again.

The elements of the industrial or mechanical control systems can be compared with the body's control system in the situation of controlling a vehicle being driven along a highway. The vision serves as sensor (3), one portion of the brain serves as the judge or comparator (4) for what is desired (staying in the proper lane) (6), the mind serves as the actuator (2) that directs energy (1) to the muscles of the arm or converters (5). Normally this control system operates so well that you are unaware of it and can think of many things while you drive without attempting to consciously steer the car.

Let us return to throwing a ball as was discussed in Chapter One. This is similar to the control used in driving the vehicle above. The placement of the body is sensed by the sense organs (3) and positioned by the muscles (5) according to the comparison by the mind (4) to the pose that has been learned (6). The energy of the body (1) is used to move the muscles (5) for the initial stance as well as the throw.

The control system of the body requires a more complex source of data, however, when what happens in the future is added to controlling the immediate body. For instance, consider the follow through discussed in Chapter One that assumes that what the arms do after the throw is important. This type of magical control might be typified by an automatic watering system for your lawn that turns on or off the water now according to when the next rain will come or how dry the lawn will be in a few days.

The Zen player and the athlete in the zone can only be described as having their control data being written by the final result of the play. This can be compared to the above automatic watering system to which is added the controlling of the water now to meet the requirements of a rain as well as the effectiveness of the water or the amount of future sunshine. In other words, what happens to the lawn or ball in the future influences what is done by the present converters. The future now controls the action of the present to some degree. This leads to the very nearly impossible situation for the brain to accept about the ball players such that if the ball is going to go off course, then how can the body be changed before the ball is released so that it will not go off course. The final motion of the ball therefore effects the data (6) that is used by the comparator (4) before the ball is hit or thrown.

This situation of the future controlling the present is, however, quite common in life although it is seldom perceived as such. The majority of people believe that what is sought for or worked for can, in fact, be found with sufficient dedication and effort even if miracles are required along the way. Dedicated humans can change their future with a proper effort in the present that then changes the future to the desired future. Is this not a common religious axiom that what one seeks one can find and that there is a power within the self that can guide, direct and overcome obstacles?

It should be noted that this book differs from the present general modern approach that believes that the self is holistic, and rather, considers the self to be made up of many separate and different elements that must be coordinated to work together just as does a complex machine. In a complex machine there is a separation of the operator of the machine from the machine itself.

One confusing aspect of describing the self as being in separate pieces is that the body and brain must be considered to be separate from *you*. *You*, in this case, become the operator of the body and brain. A simple example of this separation is when you experience the attempt to change your mind or the way that you are thinking. This book uses this same approach in describing the setting of various control systems as is done when you change your mind. In other words, *you* become the operator of your own mind and body and set the functioning of the various control elements of the body and brain.

This book will not discuss the inner control processes of the body such as the controls for varying the heartbeat, breathing rate, hormone secretion, etc. These control processes do have all of the above elements of control, but since the data is generally genetic in nature and not consciously generated, they will not be discussed.

CHAPTER FOUR
THE ENERGY

One fundamental aspect of energy needs to be understood before considering the energy of the body and mind. Energy needs to be seen as a mystical entity that in its virgin or non-manifested form is completely mysterious and unknown. It can, however, take on many different natures when it becomes manifest. As an example, the hidden energy in oil can be released by burning the oil. The released energy, in the form of heat, can then be changed to generating steam in a boiler. The energy in the steam can then be changed to mechanical energy in a turbine and then finally into electrical energy when the turbine drives a generator. The energy in the body is just as variable in its form as in the above illustration except that the body starts with burning food rather than oil.

The next step in understanding energy is to understand that it is absolutely required for any change, and when choosing energy for a specific change, the following questions must be answered:

1. What type of energy is required?
2. How much total energy is required?
3. What rate is required in using the energy (power)?

Experience has told you that the energy of the sun will not directly supply the energy for an individual to climb a mountain nor can a cup of sugar power an automobile. If you want heat from a fireplace, logs must be burned. Physical muscular energy cannot help you to change your mind or to solve a problem, rather some type of mental energy must be expended.

The required amount of energy is easy to understand since it is always proportional to the amount of change that is desired or required. The energy required to select your breakfast cereal certainly does not require as much energy as the decision to start a new career. The energy to brush your teeth does not take as much energy as the energy required to shovel snow from your walks in winter. Similarly, the energy to solve your problem in an overdrawn bank account may take more energy than what you would have used in shoveling snow, and understanding this book may take more energy than balancing your account.

The rate of supplying energy or the power that is used is essential in effectuating change. For instance, you may have sufficient logs to heat your room for an evening, but if you limit the rate or power of the burning such that the logs will last all week, you probably will be very unsatisfied with the resulting rate of heat liberated. Similarly, if you attempt to change your understanding of some subject by the expenditure of energy in reading, but limit the power of study to reading only one sentence a week, by the time you finish your study, you will have forgotten the bulk of the material. In personal change, a critical amount of energy and a critical rate of expending that energy is required.

At the turn of the last century, physiologists considered that there were two basic forms of energy within the body, a basic source of energy obtained from food that powered the physical and mental operations of the body and a higher form of energy called the *élan vital* or *anima*. The higher form of energy was assumed to determine the self-healing power of individuals as well as their higher creative power or capabilities. This higher energy was obtained by the conversion of food energy similar to the conversion of oil into electrical power. The chief function of physicians and clergy was to increase the *élan vital* so that an individual could rise above the sickness and limitations of the physical world (Becker & Seldon, 1985, pp. 25-29).

You experience the rising of the higher energy when you face some extra demand upon your body and mind such as having to speak to a group of people or solve some problem. You may, for instance, describe it as having to find the proper mood or to psych yourself up. One interesting modern view of the *anima* or the healing energy is that it is strongest in the patients who complain and question the modern mechanistic medical institution and is weakest in those who blindly submit. Another example of the higher energy is found on your good days when you can do no wrong, and whatever you attempt to do gets changed and completed. You probably described this state as being filled with a special energy.

Our modern society persists in believing that the answer to change lies in the outer physical world. You change yourself with a pill, with a developmental program, a retreat, confession of your sins, or prayer. Individuals are taught to try harder if nothing else works. This concept may start in grade school when little Johnny finds that the teachers become happy with his performance when he screws up his face, holds his breath and grunts as he pays attention. Little Sally, who is relaxed in the back row yet carefully assimilating every thought, may be considered to be listless and inattentive in class. Similarly, adults are impressed with the friendly outgoing salesperson who is enthusiastic and expressive. Your conditioned response is that this person is highly knowledgeable and honest while the quiet, shy salesperson is greatly distrusted.

Trying to do something with no results can be explained with a similar problem encountered in science. You know, for instance, that sugar contains a high concentration of energy, but if you try to release this energy by holding a sugar cube and then trying to ignite it with a match or even a torch, you fail. All that will happen is that the sugar might char slightly or melt, but there will be no sudden flame or ignition. The opposition to the release of the energy in sugar is very similar to your personal release of energy to clean out a closet that for some reason meets with opposition each time you try to get started on cleaning it.

Science calls this opposition to sugar burning or closet cleaning a barrier potential. To overcome the barrier potential a special or higher form of energy is required. As for instance, if the sugar cube is first dipped into some ashes, it will then ignite quite easily. In the case of cleaning the closet, you might suddenly find a catalyst when the phone rings and you find that you will have a weekend visitor who will need to use that closet. The closet is then easily and quickly cleaned.

It is easy to see why this barrier is necessary, since if it were not there all possible changes might take place immediately. All food and fuel would certainly immediately burst into flame. All of those productive thoughts and actions that you have avoided might suddenly pour forth and your body would then be overwhelmed in attempting to do everything at once. Barrier potentials exist to stabilize the world including your own inner world. The energy that can overcome this barrier is, however, a different type of energy from that involved with the final or actual activity. The energy that overcomes potentials is a special form of a higher energy that is necessary in creation or innovation.

Science and Religion are both to be blamed for the denial of this special higher creative energy. Science, in attempting to be removed from any stigma of religion, has been very careful to give the image of being strictly materialistic. Past scientific publications generally avoided any spiritual or mystical dissertations. Einstein, as one of the exceptions, certainly received immediate criticism when he pointed out that the basic elements and building blocks of science, namely energy, space, and time were, in fact, mystical elements. Psychology likewise attempted to be concerned only with the measurable aspects of individuals and consequently had to drop the study of consciousness, since consciousness was found to be an abstract concept and unable to be directly measured. Instead, Psychology concentrated upon measurable behavior.

Religion, on the other hand, has had to develop a concept of reality based upon belief rather than material evidence. Religion took the position that belief verifies what is real and therefore tangible proof is meaningless and perhaps actually misleading. Religion also had the problem of recognizing the power of belief on one hand and then denying belief on the other. Individual religions faced the problem that they were built upon belief, yet their members should not believe what other religions taught or else they might join the other groups. This problem was overcome with dogma that was unique to each religion. Belief was therefore limited to believing dogma.

Since a religious institution also required that all of its members believe the same reality, any new creations could not be considered but rather only the original creation. In most religions, the ability to create was also lacking in the priesthood, who were only able to interpret the past manifesting of the original creative powers.

At the moment, there are no large institutions that teach or accept the concept of an inner creative energy. The reason for this is obvious since the institutions must maintain their position of authority. Each college, church or political group is formed around a particular view that is not open to moderation or addition. Creativity is not a desirable trait in members of an institution. Industry is no exception, despite their claims that they look for creative people. Industry perhaps even more than other organizations requires conformance to existing rules and concepts. There are a number of ancient writings[8] that describe the inner energy that is used for creative or supernormal[9] activities; however, many of these have been distorted by very biased translations. One common example is the shifting of

[8] See Peck (1998) Chapter 1 for the power of ancient writings.
[9] See Peck (1999) Chapter 1 for a discussion of supernormal powers.

phrases like, “inner power (of the individual)” to “inner power of the church.”

The remainder of this book will discuss the methods of unlocking the inner creative energy to produce changes. In general, it is associated with restlessness of the lower abdomen such as commonly seen in excited children. You have experienced the source of creative energy during some traumatic situation when you experienced churning or wrenching of your guts. The ancients argued that this gut wrenching produced a higher form of energy that could then be used to power supernormal activities. Many of the advanced exercises in the martial arts or Indian Yoga attempt to develop this capability of the body so that it can be more readily available in normal tasks. Our modern view of the body, however, states erroneously that this inner tension or activity is bad and should be sedated with drugs or diversion-type activities. Our society does not welcome, support or encourage supernormal or creative activities in its members.

CHAPTER FIVE
THE ACTUATOR

This chapter deals with an element of control called the actuator that you are quite familiar with, which you no doubt call your willpower. The will to do something is normally veiled in mystery as you are unsure what affects it. At times it appears quite strong even without much effort on your part and then at other times, no matter what you try, it seems dead. Hopefully, this chapter can give you an explanation and an understanding that will allow you to find and use your will-power.

Essentially the actuator turns on the power that is necessary to do some task, whether it is thinking or something physical. One of the first requirements of the actuator and perhaps one of its hardest tasks is to turn on the power or energy to overcome the barrier potential discussed in the last chapter.

The actuator can be described simply as the device or control element that regulates the power that will be applied to the converters or the elements that convert the power into the desired end result. The body's actuator controls the energy flow or the power that will be directed to the muscles as well as how much energy will be directed to the brain and thinking.

In terms of mechanical control systems, the actuator may be a simple switch that can turn on or off a heater, a light or some electrical appliance. It might also be a dimmer switch that turns a light on and off as well as setting how bright it will be. It may also be a speed control for a motor or an accelerator pedal in an automobile or a valve that turns on and off the flow of water.

In terms of the human body, the actuator is that part of you that first energizes your selected control system and then releases the proper energy to the muscles or brain. The actuator is of course, limited by the comparator such that the desired results specified by the data can be obtained. As an example, there are many things that you could be doing, feeling or thinking about, but the actuator only energizes the few control systems that are required or desired. Once the data for your control system is selected, the actuator then increases or decreases the flow of energy such that the goal is obtained.

As already mentioned, the actuator is synonymous with what is called the *will.* If you do not have any will to clean out the garage, the muscles will not respond to the task. Similarly, if you do not use the actuator or will to send energy to your brain, you cannot think. It is interesting that the source of power is generally blamed for not thinking about something rather than the will. In our modern society it seems preferable to say that you do not have the energy or power to do something rather than to say that you do not have sufficient will to turn on the muscles or brain. The difference between wanting to do something and the will to do something gets blurred.

The actuator or will of the body seems to have another aspect to it that is independent from what you think you are supposed to do or even what you want to do. The body and brain can be all set to do some task, yet the will does not turn on the necessary flow of energy to do the work. The will seems to be dependent upon something beyond the immediate tasks to be performed. The absence of the will or actuator is also found in dreaming that includes daydreaming, as well as in many drug induced states. In these dream-type states, you have no ability to choose or dedicate to or change your future. Your comparator is also turned off or turned down since your outer senses have generally been turned off. About the only control that you do have is the ability to add to your basic temporary data to make the dream state consistent, as for instance creating a car in a parking lot if you have to have transportation. In dream states your actuator or will is turned off and you feel the lack of having any personal control.

You are, of course, also aware of the reverse when the will is willing to turn on the power to do something, yet the power is sluggish and the muscles seem fatigued and listless like after an illness or prior exertion.

Other times, the power and will may be ready, yet the data is incomplete such as when you would like to play some musical instrument that you have never tried before. The will may be fully on and the body's energy and the muscles ready to play some complex musical piece, yet the data is not developed or sufficient. Your lack of will is most noticeable and apparent when your data says that the job to be done is going to be long, arduous, and boring. Then your will or actuator seems to be the chief limiting element.

The will or actuator is driven by dedication; the more that you are dedicated to a particular direction to go, the greater the will to go. Similarly, if someone wants you to do some work that you are not interested in doing or have no dedication to do, the will and hence the physical output are likewise low. Individuals who have a strong dedication are a marvel to others, as they seem to have boundless energy as they endeavor to achieve their goals.

Religion lauds the power of the will as being a god-like force in individuals. Indeed, it really is the basis for evolution in that it is essential for the seeking of answers in life and in overcoming your bonds of conditioning.

CHAPTER SIX
THE SENSORS

The response of an individual to exterior stimulation is not clearly understood. For instance, how do you explain the situation when you hear things that don't exist and do not hear things that do exist, such as hearing threatening sounds at night or not hearing traffic sounds. Why is it that a number of people observing an accident offer such different and many times conflicting eyewitness accounts? You also may sense the subtle mood or feelings of someone with whom there is little normal sensory contact, such as sensing an anger in a person walking past you at work who outwardly appears no different than on other days. Similarly, you sometimes sense that what you are about to do is wrong and should be avoided, which at times turns out to be true and at other times very false. As mentioned before, you may have sensed an attraction to some person, place or event that later proved to have offered invaluable information to you days later.

In general, modern society and its conditioning limit the response of your sense organs. In your normal world, the levels of your outer sensors are set according to the prescribed limits for some conditioned role or response. This limitation is necessary in order to perform your conditioned tasks, since otherwise you would become distracted by unwanted sense perceptions such as the sound of traffic or conversations while attempting to listen to a phone conversation. Children are taught this ability to set the inner controls of their sense organs in school as they sit attentive at their desks facing the teacher and ignoring their fellow students and other distractions. Habituation further limits the sensory response, and soon you become immune to the smell of garbage for instance, if you work with garbage. Every job or social encounter has its built-in or conditioned acceptable limits of sensory response.

There is, however, a very wide and largely unknown range in sensory output that can be found if societal conditioning is overcome. This increase in sensory performance is impossible to describe in terms of modern materialistic modeling, and so this chapter will introduce a very ancient model that is able to more nearly provide a working model to understand and then control your world. In order to fully introduce the ancient model, it is first necessary to review the wide range of sensory perceptions. Almost everyone is aware of the increased sensitivity of the physical senses such as the auditory compensation of the blind or the increased finger sensitivity of a surgeon, but there is an even greater range of sensory response that is of even greater importance than that of the physical sense organs. This increased functioning is labeled as subtle.

The subtle nature of the sensory system is easily introduced with the sensory inputs obtained in dreams or altered states of consciousness. Many of these subtle sense perceptions from within the mind can be explained as the sensing of external sounds or vibrations coupled with the recreation of scenes from memory. There are also imaginary or subtle sense perceptions that seemingly are triggered by some past remembrance or thought related to the immediate experienced world. As for example, some dream experience may recreate some feelings from the past giving rise to the sense of an unreal yet potent smell that permeates your present world, or your present world may suddenly appear to be tinged in a rosy glow coupled with some vague undefined remembrance. There is also the unexplained sensory input that arrives in mental states that can be classified as *altered* in which your immediate actions are suddenly perceived as incomprehensible and alien. Similarly, sensory input that doesn't physically exist, such as hearing a voice of warning or a bright light, can be perceived.

One common experience of the mystical nature of the senses is found in conversation wherein you are intent upon conveying some teaching or message to someone else and suddenly recognize intense warnings to avoid introducing some new topic. As for instance, you find yourself about to mention divorce and find an inner sense not to pursue this subject. Later you may find that the person you were addressing was in the midst of a painful divorce proceeding that you were unaware of.

Powerful actors and actresses cite how they require the subtle sense of the audience and must play to that sense. This sense is obviously not normally obtained with the five normal physical senses, since the audience is hidden behind the stage lights and they must keep their focus upon their fellow actors.

There is also a sense perception found to link minds together, to some extent, such as when you suddenly understand fully what your companion is desiring to tell you before the details are even expressed. The engineering school at Princeton performed some very well-controlled experiments to prove that human minds can, in fact, be coupled to interact together such that one person can perceive the general view of another (Jahn, et al. 1997). This was done by one person describing what another hidden person was looking at. The results were not instantaneous but required time. It is as if the receiver has a lot of random images that pop up like noise, but if the random thought is synchronous with the sender, then that image becomes more dominant. The process therefore can proceed no faster than the generation and then synchronization of images between the two experimenters. These experiments demonstrated a greater range in interaction between humans than that obtained by a human to machine interaction, as will be discussed.

There is another comparable interrelationship in the physical world that can be useful in understanding how your senses can couple with those of others and your world. This relationship can be characterized as an observed synchronicity of events (Peat 1987). It is known for instance, that if two pendulums are adjusted to have nearly the same frequency of swing, a point is reached when they will suddenly become locked together swinging completely in unison from some small unknown coupling mechanism. When this happens, there is an energy exchange as one increases and the other decreases such that the change is paid for in energy. Synchronicity is also to be noted in conversations when you attempt to convince others of your ideas and then suddenly you all seem to have an instant agreement. Synchronicity can explain how something you need seems to appear when required. It is as if your whole world acts with some strong sensory coupling such that everything effects everything else to some degree.

All of the above sensory responses can be explained with the ancient model given in the appendix. This model assumes that there is an additional set of subtle sense organs. These organs respond to non-manifested, imagined, future sensory responses or the feelings of others. The functioning of the subtle sense organs is generally perceived as no different than that from your five sense organs. In other words, your mind is many times incapable of determining the source of a sense perception, whether it is from the physical or the subtle sense organs. As an example, you hear a sound in the middle of the night and are not capable of determining if it was real or imagined until the sound is repeated. You may also suddenly have the strong feeling that you should not cross a street and question the source and validity of that feeling, until suddenly a fast-moving car careens around the corner.

The above discussion on the variability of the senses and their different sources can now be seen as very important to the understanding of the control system as well as its ultimate mastery. Your control system cannot operate well if it contains false or inaccurate sensory inputs that are describing the world to be controlled. For instance, how can you respond to some-one's directions if your ears do not accurately hear their directions, or even worse, suppose you only hear what you want to hear?

The variability of the sense organs needs to be further elaborated upon, since the sensitivity or acuity as well as the accuracy of the organs can shift. Everyone is familiar with the alteration in the outer sense organs during extreme fear or anger where false as well as heightened sensory perceptions can be readily experienced. Your expectations of the future are also known to affect the degree of activity of your sense organs. They can range from being almost inactive with the expectations of something uninteresting to being in a hypersensitive state with the expectation of something very pleasing. Similarly, if you are expecting to hear something derogatory you will hear it, or if you expect to see something beautiful you likewise will see it.

Another source of sensory input for control is with the variable ability to sense the mood or state of another person generally explained in our modern world as a *sensitive* observation of the other person. You are conditioned to note such things as flickering eyelashes or fingers which you have learned are associated with various emotions or even occupations. Arthur Conan Doyle made this deductive analysis famous in his Sherlock Holmes stories. You are not normally aware of the input of these subtle clues, but you notice your confusion in conversing with someone wearing dark glasses or bundled tightly up in thick clothes.

This sensitive sensing is certainly a questionable perception in today's materialistic society, but so also is the question as to what is seen. The seeing is generally described as *knowing* in which the entire state of the person is known rather than some particular that might be irritating to them. In other words, you may suddenly find yourself knowing that Sally is feeling insulted without any outward clues or any awareness of just what is insulting her. It is important to note, that you do not read her mind, but rather perceive her as a total force or state. One model that is in agreement with this text is that you perceive the role that Sally is playing much as a child reacts to another child playing Queen. Your reaction would probably be accepted by your ancestors if you were to state that you are sensing the spirit of Sally with the subtle organs of sense.

The ability of the sensory system to respond to an outer world is even further extended with an inner reconstruction based upon verbal descriptions. For instance, if someone describes some past experience, if you exert yourself, you can picture what they are describing and find the feelings that are being recalled. Again, if you break free of your own interpretation of what is being said and instead allow the other person's role or spirit to interact upon you, you will share the experience as your soul touches the spirit behind the other person. This ability is again similar to children playing imaginary games together such as describing some scary tunnel that they are imagining. They can all become terrified at some common imagined threat, although they may all later describe it somewhat differently.

The sensing of the future has already been introduced with athletes who manage to find the proper exertion of the mind to reach the zone. This knowing of the future is described as the same type of knowing of others described above. The reaching of this *knowing* state requires a special energy that is described in Chapter Twenty.

There is also another model of describing this knowing as finding a *taste* of the future or the *smell* of someone's emotions or state of their mind. The ancients used the words *taste* and *smell* in describing these senses since they are indistinct and difficult to identify. These sensors have been associated with the functioning of the right hemisphere of the brain[10].

---

[10] See Peck (1976) Chapter 1 for a good overview of the right brain.

The inner sensors are also susceptible to what others do. As an example of how these sensors can be externally controlled, observe what happens when you watch someone yawn or listen to someone with a productive cough. Invariably, you find the need to yawn or cough. Similarly, an itch can develop watching someone scratch or by thinking of poison ivy or insect bites. You can see things that are not there or hear nonexistent sounds with sufficient fear or alarm. The sense of smell is very easy to vary. You may for instance, smell smoke if someone mentions fire, smell flowers if someone mentions beauty or smell sweat if you see someone perspiring. These smells may or may not agree with what others around you smell.

The sense organs are also dependent upon the role or situation that you are placed in. In play, children (and adults) can sense feelings within their bodies that are nonphysical, such as a child playing a hunchback can feel a distortion of the back. You for instance, can readily ignore your headache if you are suddenly confronted with some demand that requires you to be strong. A child playing a wounded soldier, on the other hand, can experience the pain of moving the imagined injured limb. Good actors and actresses are able to feel what their role calls for such as burning with fever, being attacked by bugs, seeing an apparition, hearing a mournful haunting sound or seeing a fellow actor as intensely handsome and attractive. The subtle inner organs of sense are of equal importance to the outer physical organs of sense but within a different level of reality. Since the subtle sense organs contributed to perceptions within subtle or imaginary worlds, the ancients labeled those subtle sense organs as belonging to the soul.

Another important consideration in using these subtle sense organs is that they can sometimes modify or replace the outer physical sensations. Hypnotists delight in demonstrating the alteration of the physical senses with hypnosis such that a hand loses its feelings or that the hand is in boiling water. Sensations arising from the gut can also appear stronger than the sensations from the physical sense organs. As for example, the smell of danger or the sensing of some presence that arises from the guts might have been important survival tools for our primitive ancestors.

It should be obvious to you that your perception of your world and self is almost completely determined by your physical and subtle sense organs that have been set early in life as well as by your desired response to the world. It should also be apparent that you are largely unaware of the source of many of your impressions of the world. This leads to the Biblical question of how can the blind lead the blind? How can you change yourself if the sensory input can only present a conditioned and fixed world and self?

The above discussion should provide you with an explanation of how and why your sense organs function as they do as well as their capability of responding at even greater levels. With this understanding and that of the other control elements it can then become possible for you to change your control system in order to create a new world and self.

CHAPTER SEVEN
THE COMPARATOR

The comparator is a mechanism that determines how precise we are. For example, in cooking, a recipe calls for a cup of milk. You may have the data that for this recipe, a great deal of variance is allowed and so you fill your measuring cup to about a full cup and take no pains to get the amount accurate. If you desire to be accurate, you must be precise and to be precise requires that the comparator be made more sensitive.

You may be using the same recipe on another day and find that you are being very precise in measuring the cup of milk even though the data says that it does not have to be accurate. You may question yourself as to why you are being so painstaking about measuring the milk today when normally you do not care. As you become aware of the situation you can touch the sense of the comparator as being an independent element in controlling your actions.

Being careful, cautious, controlled, precise, meticulous, or fastidious are states that require a sensitive and active comparator. The comparator is a single element that is set for all that occurs. When you find yourself being meticulous about your cooking or your desk for instance, you find that you are also meticulous about the other activities in your life. The reverse is also true of course when you are sloppy and careless.

The opposite state of the comparator is evidenced when it does not reject anything or will accept anything. This state of an inactive comparator is found in children learning new subjects and is described as having a pure and open mind. The comparator is also turned off in reading fiction or watching fanciful movies etc. Religion generally requires an inactive comparator in terms of accepting dogma and doctrine and call that state believing.

Mentally healthy individuals have the ability to turn the comparator on or off; however, severe problems can result if the comparator cannot be turned back on after being turned off. As an example, if a child cannot distinguish between fiction and reality, he might believe that he can fly and attempt to fly off of a high roof, or he might attempt to stop an oncoming car with magic.

The comparator is also the element that determines how closely you will work to reach some goal or the level of perfection that you require in performing some operation. For instance, you may attempt to handwrite a note. If it is on a card to a loved one, your comparator is very active as you carefully draw each letter so that it compares closely to how your data describes the perfect letter to be. On the other hand, the note may be just to remind you later to do something, in which case your comparator is turned on only enough that you can identify the letters later.

The comparator keeps you on track so that you can finish some task. The comparator determines constantly whether your thoughts and actions are directed toward the finishing of the tasks as described by the data. If the comparator is turned off, however, such as when you are not really concerned or dedicated to finishing a task, you generally find yourself distracted by one thing after another. On the other hand, you may be so dedicated to finishing some task such as reading an article, that you cannot be distracted at all, even by the ringing of the phone.

For another example, imagine that you have been asked to give a party. You have the data for a perfect party in your mind, with the guests behaving in a certain way, the decorations being beautiful, the food irresistible, the games attractive to everyone, etc. You then set out to prepare for the party. Sometime before the party is to begin, you find yourself overwhelmed with details that are not done, you have so many things to do that you are exhausted and still the party preparations are not ready. The problem is that your comparator has been so busy that nothing is satisfactory and hence nothing gets done.

The comparator also functions as your conscience. You may be tempted to do something that you would describe as questionable since you have data that says that it is bad to do it and also other data that says that it would be fun. You can feel the results of the comparators action with the inner tensions of the body as it switches back and forth between 'should' and 'shouldn't.' What generally happens at this stage is the changing of the data by giving more support to the 'should' or 'shouldn't' until the comparator can accept the comparison between the data and the proposed activity.

You may experience the comparator when you are trying to describe some insight or concept that is just taking shape in your mind. The problem comes in finding words that the comparator will accept as fully describing the insight. You discover an inner turmoil as your brain searches for something that at the deeper level of the creative mind seems quite clear. Your comparator reviews your conscious mental description with the subtle vision or idea and depending upon its sensitivity or your desire for perfection, it will either accept a poor description or keep searching.

The comparator can be easily perceived in operation as you attempt to remember something. Consider for instance, when you have forgotten someone's name and then scan a list of names to try to recall it. You also might forget how to spell a word and then write out what you think it is in order to see if it is spelled correctly. The name or spelling that you were attempting to remember suddenly comes forth with the knowledge that it is correct. In this case the comparator is in good operating condition, but the original data was perhaps weak.

The function of the comparator is hidden in the modern world under the generalized term of the "subconscious"; however, this name does little to provide a working model of how to use it much less what it is. When the comparator is understood, however, you find an increasing awareness of what really is going on in your subconscious.

CHAPTER EIGHT
THE CONVERTERS

In attempting to change yourself and your world, it is easy to ignore and not fully understand the muscles and brain that do the final work. The muscles and brain are converters that convert one form of energy into another form of energy. Muscles convert food energy into the energy of motion. The brain functions as a converter when it changes subtle images, sensory inputs, or feelings into words or labels. Most of the time, the converters work in unison such that the entire body is capable of playing a specific individualistic role. However, if they do not work in harmony, then tensions result and you suddenly become very much aware of some difficulty in your converters.

The converters or muscles of the body receive commands from three different sources that must be understood to fully control the motion of the body.

1. There is the conscious source from the brain that allows you to deliberately move your various muscles or converters,
2. the source that comes from conditioned or learned responses that go directly to the muscles, and
3. the subtle source of the subconscious action of the actuator that seems to prepare you for something in the future such as a threat or desired result.

The operation of the muscle converters under conscious mental control is well understood as the brain creates temporary data as to what the converters are to do. This conscious control allows you to do new things such as to bend over and pick something up, sing a new song, analyze problems, or greet a stranger.

The second source of command is evidenced with athletes who spend considerable time training their muscles or converters to respond without conscious control as do people driving in traffic, musicians, artists, and assembly line production workers. Many mental jobs are also the result of conditioned learning and response such as basic arithmetic, reading, and speaking. In these cases, the muscles or brain cells are generally trained by consciously moving those converters in the manner that will be required to repeat later. The resulting data from this training is then immediately accessible to the converter element of the control system and does not have to go through the conscious comparator or actuator.

Many times, the conditioned directions to the muscles seem to be within the muscles themselves. For instance, it is as if the control mechanism resides within the arms of a boxer as the boxer responds faster than would be expected. The response time is thus faster than the expected time it would take for a mental neural command to reach the arms from the brain. Similarly, students who master special Eastern energizing techniques can respond more than twice as rapidly as others when they are taught to find an inner physical response system other than their brains.[11]

The subtle senses provide the third connection for directing or commanding the converters, which is normally considered as resulting in impulsive or subconscious responses. You may unexpectedly speak, move or think without any conscious effort to do so. You are familiar with the sudden statement you might make during some conversation or confrontation that was entirely unexpected. You also may have found that you stepped aside just in time to protect yourself from some falling object without any volitional input. In addition, you may find yourself opening a book and reading some passage without knowing the

---

[11] See Peck (1998) Appendix A: *Response Time for Tantriks*

reason. This unexpected overriding of your normal conditioned control system can perhaps later be attributed to the underlying dedication that is in place at the time, particularly if something is gained from reading the book that is needed the next day.

The developing of the subtle sense data can sometimes be experienced during interactions with others such as during a party when you let yourself go. You may find yourself dancing in some new manner with someone, or telling stories that you would never consciously tell. Your converters seem to be controlled somehow by the demands of the party. Similarly, a good salesman will find that his body and voice take on a characteristic that is conducive to overpowering a potential customer.

Yoga has a name for this control by the subtle senses called *samyama* which means "controlling together." Good dancers learn to let their converters move according to their partners' motions as if one body controls both bodies. This mutually controlled response can be described as the merger of their individually trained converters as well as the coupling of their subtle or physical sense organs.

The modern world suffers from what can be called tensions that result from converters attempting to respond to the different sources all at once. As an example, you meet someone who is perceived to be dangerous or obnoxious, yet you must be polite and considerate because of some social convention. Your muscles tighten up ready to defend yourself or to run away, yet you can do neither as the conscious conditioned mind forces the muscles to hold a normal stance or posture. Similarly, you may have to give a report that you do not wish to give, your muscles desire to run free of the encounter while they are also forced to walk to the meeting. The cognitive brain suffers from the same type of tensions as it may wish to think about a problem related to a child at home while you are at work, yet at the same time your brain is also forced to think about the needs of an immediate customer.

The converters must be ready to function at any time and hence remain tense as long as any data requires some action or response. Tensions can therefore only be diminished by changing your data.

CHAPTER NINE
DATA

This chapter is perhaps the most important part of the book since it deals with the essential criteria for defining the desired change or control limits. Data can be defined as that which describes what you and the perceived outer world should be under particular conditions. The brain must be able to create or find the data that describes a desired future that the control system needs to conform to. For example, you need an accurate picture of what type of clothing others will be wearing at an upcoming party in order to plan for your own future dress. This data must be complete enough so that at each unfolding moment the comparator can compare what is supposed to be from what is actually being experienced.

There are four types of data that you use:

- genetic,
- conditioned,
- temporary and
- *gnosis* or knowledge.

Genetic data is that data that is present at birth and includes DNA coding, experiences obtained in the womb, and perhaps as some religions and philosophies argue, the experiences gained from prior existence.

Conditioned data is that which is gained from the repeated and reinforced training and education received from family and society. It includes what is commonly called wisdom or habit.

Temporary data is imaginative or formative and is used to provide data for the development of fully brand-new operational data. Temporary data is also used to create new roles to be played.

Gnosis (Greek) means “to know” in the sense of touching truth or some intuition or insight that was not previously known. *Gnosis* is knowledge (early definition) as distinguished from the data called wisdom.

The complexity of genetic data and its wide range of descriptions is becoming better understood as more and more deficiencies of individuals are found to be related to their DNA coding. This chapter will not expand upon genetic data other than to point out how the DNA data works as an example of other sources of data as well as some of the internal conflicts arising from other data.

A DNA molecule furnishes its data to surrounding control centers by duplicating its structure in RNA molecules that then move away from the chromosome into outlying regions of the containing cell. This might be compared with making a photocopy of a cookbook in a library and then carrying the photocopy home as data to prepare meals.

A similar source of data is found with the genetic data contained in hormones. Hormones are generated and then serve as data when they find an open receptor that fits their particular shape, whereupon they can then transfer their data much as the RNA molecule does.

DNA, as well as being the source of biological and instinctual data, is also the source of basic societal data such as manifested in the need to fight for your own existence in a group. This societal data includes being sure that you get in line for food and at the head of the line if possible. On the other hand, although the data obtained from DNA and societal conditioning forces you to desire to be at the head of the group, you also desire to be accepted within the group by conforming. This conflicting data also appears within an infant who wants quick satisfaction to hunger pains, but also does not want to be rejected. Infants learn quickly to modify their cries between demanding/controlling and helplessness/conformance.

Conditioned data, even though it is generally built upon DNA data, is even more conflicting. For almost every bit of data that says, for instance, that you should be positive, you have an equal amount of data saying that you should be negative. If you consider the data of being successful, you give rise to the opposing data that you are not better than anyone else, or that it will take too much effort. If you have data of being friendly to strangers, other data immediately appears and says that you might get mugged or robbed. If you attempt to use the data of feeling good, the opposite data appears pointing to the dangers of feeling good or of becoming threatening to your somber friends.

Problems also arise when what you see on the outside does not agree with what is desired on the inside. For instance, you may believe that you are being a kind person yet others state that you are being unkind. Similarly, your inner feelings may not agree with what you believe your feelings should be. In general, strong feelings in the bowels are conditioned to be bad, while those in the head or brain are labeled as good if they agree with religious or moral teachings that you have received from childhood. This combination of do/don't commands or data is fundamental in understanding individual control.

This do/don't or supportive/opposing data is used by control engineers to keep a machine or operation within tight limits. If the machine, for instance, operates too efficiently then opposing data is introduced to slow it down, or if it is operating below the standard then a supportive set of data is compared. Society uses the same type of conflicting data to keep its members in their proper places. You have one set of data that you use when you are hungry and another set of data that you use when you are full. These two sets of data keep you from starving as well as from over eating. Similarly, you use one set of data in being friendly with people but another set of data that keeps you from being a bore or dominating other people.

Humans are unique in the animal world in that they have a much longer period of time to be infants and children and hence are able to more fully develop their minds and become more conditioned to a complex society. However, this data gained by prolonged conditioning or learning may not be consciously recognized. As an example, in tying your shoe, you rely upon data that seems to be stored in your fingers and find that it is nearly impossible to describe how to tie your shoes, but generally you must resort to physically tying the knots. Parents in helping their children to tie their shoes will invariably stand behind the child so that they can tie the child's shoe as if it were their own. Similarly, there are times when you cannot verbally describe some operation to someone else, but must revert to showing how it is done.

Professional people rely upon conditioned data to do their jobs. One interesting example of gaining conditioning is the tradition of physician internship. They are forced to go without much sleep and yet respond to life and death matters. Doctors facing prolonged emergencies do not have to think and instead can rely upon their conditioning gained through years of training to meet some immediate challenge.

Conditioned verbal data is stored and retrieved in many ways, such as evidenced when you are asked what letter comes before 'X.' In general most people will have to subvocalize or recite at least part of the memorized alphabet since they do not have a learned response to the position of single letters. Similarly, you may have to recite your whole social security number to state the last four digits. The ancients required children to memorize prose or songs to inject voluminous data into children and is still evidenced as children sing their ABC's.

You can be very aware of very fundamental inner conditioned controlling data if you watch your own responses to the outer world. Most of these responses are automatic such as the manner in which you laugh. Each family has slight variations in laughing that are conditioned. The manner in which you speak, walk and how you stand are all conditioned. Your preferences for food, manner of approaching problems, gestures, or social interactions with others are determined by conditioning, both from the family as well as from your immediate society.

Added to this early societal conditioning is the conditioning of being different people or rather of playing different roles. For instance, a child must be a different person in a schoolroom than when on the playground with friends or with a grandparent. Each different role requires a separate data bank that may of course include some of the same data as in other roles, but nonetheless, the data must all fit together to define the role. For instance, you cannot keep the data of squealing with delight from the playground and use it in the classroom data bank. The data in each role must all be consistent with that role.

Wisdom should also be recognized as basic conditioned data and you are aware of its accumulation as you had to memorize such things as your phone number, the content of books and the proper behavior in various situations. This data or your wisdom includes your developed arguments or rationality for such things as your religious or political views and lifestyle.

Wisdom can be categorized as being made up of three types of data: scientific, belief and false. Scientific data is that data that can be verified or proven. Belief data is data that cannot or will not be proven. False data or false wisdom can be proven wrong yet continues in society primarily to support some false position of an individual or institution. Some ancient writings laud those who have the ability to discriminate or to identify belief and false data for what they are.

Temporary data is used in determining what data can or should be used in finding a control. Temporary data is commonly used in analysis or in developing some new concept where the end goal may be known but the underlying data is not. For instance, in attempting to explain some observation of the outer world, you search for data that might support or explain the observation. During this process your mental control system becomes busy substituting temporary data into the mental converter to find data to best describe the observation.

As an example, Bill is perceived to have made some unusual facial expression and you are attempting to understand the meaning behind it. Your brain or mental control system tries to analyze what is behind his facial expression by applying one definition after another to the perceived expression such as starting with, "Is he angry?" But perhaps that does not fit so your mind finds another possible definition such as, "Is he happy?" That definition may not fit, so another definition is compared and so forth until the comparator finds some agreement. When your comparator does find a comparison, you then accept that Bill's immediate expression indicates frustration and that conclusion becomes permanent data.

There is another form of temporary data that is used in taking on another role to be played. The best example of this is the data that is used by a child in a make-believe game such as playing the part of a magical princess. The child does not have any permanent data as to how to be a princess and must first assume some temporary data and then see how that data fits into the game. Parents also use this type of temporary data in teaching their children to become civilized.

For instance, parents will give a child the temporary data of being a good girl and then coach the child into being able to fully play that role just as a child would experience in an imaginary game. Upon forced repetition, this temporary data becomes permanent and the child labels it as the data of being good. Similarly, you may be given a position of authority and you then assume new or temporary data that describes your new role or position. After months of playing that role, the data becomes conditioned and the role is automatically put on when you step into the place requiring it.

The concept of *gnosis* or knowledge as data was expressed in early psychology as *conation* before they excluded any non-measurable phenomena. Conation was described as pre-thought or precognition. The basic idea is that before you can have a thought about something, you must first have a feeling of that something. Your conscious thinking process then attempts to put concrete words and definitions to that feeling. To the early Greek philosophers, *gnosis* or knowledge, was built upon feelings that were called *eidos* or word[12]. Word therefore contained only the essence of something before it became classified or called by name. As an example, you identify a table in many forms because behind any table is a feeling of *tableness* or of that something with a level flat surface. Some religions speak of creation coming forth first as a word or the basic feeling of what is to be. Then it is made manifest. Similarly, you first have a subtle feeling of what might be and then you make it manifest by putting actual physical words to it.

In terms of common experience, at times you can be aware of the required mental effort as you attempt to describe some inner feeling or insight. This inner effort is of the mental control system that converts the subtle to the gross or the conative to the cognitive. You perceive this inner mental control system working as you experience the rejection by your comparator as it fails to find a corresponding word to express the inner feeling.

[12] Ibid. Chapter 12: *Knowledge, Truth, and the Word*

You may, for instance, apologize and state that what you are saying doesn't quite fit what you are feeling. Similarly, you may spend time attempting to clarify some mental image you cannot quite see clearly. The accuracy of your descriptions or how well they fit your subtle feelings depends upon the sensitivity of your mental comparator. Clarity in thinking or cognition requires a sensitive comparator and control system in order to convert subtle data into definitive words. Controlling the comparator will be discussed later in Chapter Seventeen.

Data from *gnosis* is generally expressed as having to be found deep within yourself. In solving a problem, you are aware of seeking some image or feeling that can lead you to some productive thought process. What is exciting is that when the data from *gnosis* is found, it appears suddenly and generally with great clarity. However, many times as you attempt to translate this instant *gnosis* into words, you discover that it takes time and effort to describe the feeling to others.

To many of the ancients, this subtle data from *gnosis* was stored in or obtained from the lowest portion of your body in what was called your Spirit (see appendix). Calling this source the Spirit fits some of your experiences as you feel that you are digging deep into the unknown as you attempt to express some feeling.

The data from *gnosis* is many times evidenced as appearing to be from the future. This data is found to be accurate and is associated generally with strong gut feelings. Many times, this data does not ever get changed into the cognitive space, but serves to supply the data for what are called the purely gut or intuitive reactive responses to life.

In conclusion, it must be remembered that your interpretation of self and world is based upon data that has many sources: genetic, temporary, conditioned or *gnosis*. These sources offer data that may not be complete or accurate and may even be false. The value of this data is determined almost solely by your dedication and your ability to discriminate as will be discussed in later chapters.

CHAPTER TEN
EXAMPLES

The following are some examples of how the various control elements operate in certain conditions.

1. One morning Lisa woke feeling that the world was not a nice place and her job in particular was boring drudgery. She glumly readied herself for getting to work and facing the day. On another morning Lisa woke with a languorous stretch and rubbed her body thinking how wonderful the world was and how lucky she was to have such a wonderful job with exciting people.

Both of these instances can be related to data. There is an old hymn entitled "When Upon Life's Billows" in which there is the prominent line, "Count your many blessings" which recognizes the value of positive good data. If you think of any blessings that you have, you force the data to change. If you start the day with a simple stretch and then let it feel good, you immediately tend to select the data that goes with a wonderful world.

2. Bill was still up long after his bedtime, struggling to understand a new corporate directive. The directive was complex, outlining the interaction of many departments and individuals, but Bill knew that it wasn't as complex as he was making it. However, the more he read, the less he could understand.

Several of the control elements are problems in this case. The first is the type of energy being used. Most people are unaware of the higher-type of energy necessary when transforming words into concepts (or concepts into words). For example, the energy that is used to walk across a room or move a chair is not going to work in transforming words into concepts such as above. One of the indications of this lack of higher energy is that the more he read the less he understood. This is like your automobile running out of gasoline, when the more you pump the accelerator the faster you seem to come to a stop. The comparator is not functioning at its best level since there is no clear signal as to what word or phrase is not making sense. The mental converter that converts words into thoughts or concepts is also not running well since it is low in higher energy.

3. Alice was slowly going nuts with the kids. They were getting into all kinds of mischief and being disrespectful to her as well. They did not seem to respond to the various games she tried to amuse them with and instead they seemed to just want to be noisy and wild.

Of course, the kids could be just wild, since they too can select different sets of data. However, it is more likely that Alice's comparator is working too hard and is too sensitive. For some reason she is far more critical of the children's behavior than on other days. It is not as if she has another set of data relating to her expectations, but rather that the children do not fully meet her old data. A common diagnosis of this condition is that Alice has lost her patience and is expecting perfection.

4. Mary stopped painting her chair and stood back wondering how she could have possibly missed so many spots with her paintbrush. True her mind was on other things, but it wasn't like her to be so sloppy.

This type of problem can be explained with a lack of activity of either the comparator or the sensors or both. The comparator relaxes and essentially says that the missed spots are good enough or the sensors are not fully turned on and actually do not see the missed spots. When Mary finished and wished to admire her work, she had to fully turn on her sensors, of course, and then the defects became obvious.

5. Then there is John and his garden. John had spent the day before working in the garden, yet nothing seemed to get done. The dirt seemed too hard to shovel and he could not find one tool after another. There were too many distractions with the dog barking and the children asking questions and the whole day then proceeded in the same manner. Today, however, he finished planting in the seed after digging, cultivating and raking in what seemed like a very short time, and what was more remarkable was that it seemed so easy, at least compared to the day before.

The first suspicion here is with the actuator or will. On the first day John's actuator restricted the flow of energy into his body and mind resulting in what could be easily classified as laziness. With a limited flow of energy, the simple act of digging can seem to be almost impossible. With the actuator turned down in terms of gardening, John also found difficulty in finding energy in other activities during the day. This suggests the initial dedication might be the source of the problem. The increased ease on the second day can be explained with the increased dedication and the turned-on actuator plus the normal relaxation that takes place after overcoming the barrier potential to the job.

6. Harry was young with only a high school education, but had managed to get a job where he was expected to think and interrelate with other people. He really liked the job and was starting to think that he might be able to take evening courses at the local University. He had been discouraged, however, in high school from going to college because he had been labeled as having a learning disability, and his grades certainly could

be construed to support that idea. He was amazed, however, after a month of taking two courses that he actually enjoyed the courses and found that his grades were near the top of his class.

Harry obtained a job with people who expected him to do more things and did not justify failure. As a result, his conditioned data of himself changed and added the data of being able to learn and respond to the outer world. With the courses, his data changed further and the old concepts of hating to study was being replaced with the expectation of success and the sense of accomplishment.

7. Jessie had a great deal of trouble with what was real. He would talk about seeing ghosts in a room or hearing voices when no one else could hear them. If he listened to a religious program that mentioned that the enlightened people could see halos around certain others, he would see halos. Those that knew him knew that he was not fabricating or lying, but that he really did think that he experienced the things that no one else would.

The problem appeared to be with his comparator and how it accepted anything close to what was desired without much discrimination. He had apparently started turning down the activity of his comparator in middle school when he missed a couple of months of school and could never catch up. His only possible method of fitting into his peer group was to accept blindly what was said and consequently he learned not to trust his own judgement and hence turned down his comparator. He also learned to increase the sensitivity of his senses in order to perceive what would be on the fringe to others. With increased visual input and less rejection by his comparator, his imagination could add to his perceived world without any limitation. His problems were finally corrected when Jessie learned how to use his comparator. He was then able to quickly sort out the real from the imagined and find the same world as those around him.

8. Tom was normally a go-getter, optimistic and energetic in all that he did. This served him well in his job that required a high degree of innovation and creativity. However, he could drop into the almost exactly opposite state very quickly and become enervated and very pessimistic. Perhaps a psychologist could have diagnosed him as being manic-depressive. One evening he noticed the sequence of events when his wife seemingly ignored him after he felt that he had put forth a great deal of effort to please her. With the real or imagined shun, he found that he quickly withdrew into himself and was not even interested in his hobby. Time seemed to drag and he felt completely without any interest in anything.

When Tom was told about his actuator or inner will, he could then very clearly see the problem as the actuator shutting down the flow of energy into his entire body and mind. When he was trying to please his wife, he was positive and optimistic with increased sensitivity of his senses and comparator. When he felt shunned by his wife, his data said that she should have been smiling and complimentary but his active comparator and senses failed to detect that. Once his control system gave him the information that he was not getting the proper response from the outer world, he withdrew by shutting down his actuator.

9. Sharon had episodes when her heartbeat would become erratic and when it did, she would feel the rise of anxiety and an increasing inability to function. An examination by her doctor could reveal no structural problems. With some help Sharon found that she did have a control over her heart rate as first evidenced by being able, despite her fears, to further increase

her heart rate. She was then asked to synchronize her heartbeat with a one second clock tick which, after some effort, she was also able to do.

The solution to her problem was seen as increasing the sensitivity of the comparator in her heart control system. By attempting to synchronize her heart with the tick, her comparator was forced into increased sensitivity as a new source of data was used. During her anxiety attack as her senses sharpened and detected a slight irregularity, her comparator would compare this increasing heart rate with her previous even more rapid heart rate rather than to her inner subtle control data. This was evidenced by her ability to speed up her heart when she changed the data from her previous attacks to that of the expectation of an even faster rate. The comparator had to become more sensitive in comparing to the audible tick of the clock and then even more sensitive to find the subtle normal heart control signal.

10. Bill became very critical of the intolerance of others toward new ideas after he joined a new religious group. This intolerance began when he found himself being rebuffed and ignored as he attempted to explain new ideas to others outside of his religious group. He tried many different approaches to convince others, but in all cases his arguments and explanations were totally ignored. His sense of superiority and separation increased until one day, an old school friend showed up and attempted to tell Bill about another religion. In the resulting confrontation, Bill lost his old friend and found himself deeply hurt.

Bill finally managed to see that the problem was with his own intolerance. When he presented his problems to an older uncle whom he greatly admired, the ensuing discussion pointed out how he clung tightly to one set of data while his comparator rejected any other data. The wise uncle suggested that Bill, rather than rejecting new or alternate concepts, first attempt to thoroughly understand the opposing ideas. This action forced his comparator to become less sensitive. After many months of diligently attempting to fully understand other beliefs, he then applied the same process to his own beliefs and started to find an increasing awareness and interest in the outer world.

11. Jan prided herself on being successful at 'controlling' her life, yet she failed to find happiness. She raised two children who became successful, she had an immaculate house, she was in excellent health, her husband appeared happy and she was active in her church. There was nothing that she lacked in terms of comfort or possessions, but she felt a vague sense of unhappiness and emptiness. At various times she had tried self-help groups and books that promised to lead to happiness. All was to no avail. What was she failing to understand and control?

Jan had truly found perfection in the world of law and society that led to her becoming satiated with life or finding the state of gluttony in terms of evolution[13]. The modern world considers gluttony as eating too much, but it has an older meaning of being satiated or having no room for further acquisition. Jan had no desire for anything more in life and all of her desires had been fulfilled. She no longer had anything to live for other than maintaining what she had.

No doubt her friends asked her why she didn't find some outside interest that would occupy her, but they could not understand that she had no need for anything more, she had everything she needed. However, this state of gluttony can quickly lead to the state of Grace with the simple act of recognizing that everything

[13] See Peck (1988) Chapter 13 for description of the ancient sin of gluttony.

that you have is in fact the fulfillment of your past desires and some guiding hand had to be recognized in finding all that you desired. Once Jan recognized the miracle of her attainment, then two things occurred. The first was the recognition of a Divine presence that allowed her to obtain anything in life that she desired. The second realization was that she had the power to choose her own future.

Jan then started to more fully appreciate what she had as being miraculous so that she started looking for even more in what she had. Secondly, she decided that she still had a long life to lead and that she could in fact start a career and so returned back to college to become a schoolteacher. She then became busy extending her data with an active actuator and a sensitive comparator.

Needless to say, Jan now speaks of the challenges of life and the joy of seeking.

BOOK TWO

CONTROLLING THE FUTURE

CHAPTER ELEVEN
CREATION OF REALITY

In order to understand the changing or creation of your own individual world and self, it is necessary to first consider the first Creation. The subject of the Creation of the human race and the universe has become an emotional issue with two major camps arguing as to its origin.

One camp argues that a god created everything without further changes and left it that way. The other camp argues that everything came about by chance over a long period of time starting with a single phenomenon and that everything is slowly decaying. Both camps do in fact have a commonality in truth that is based upon an initial Creation and a controlling Law. This can be seen with a bit of common sense and a bit of reading between the lines.

Unfortunately, both claims lead you quickly to a very pessimistic view of your life and your personal future since you are either only following a prepared script or are no different than a weed. However, suppose that you are somehow a part of the creation process and capable of further creation? This gives rise to a more optimistic third camp view that argues for an even more fundamental explanation of creation as will be described. The appendix gives an ancient description of a control system of the third camp that exists within an individual rather than within a god or chance.

As a general introduction to creation consider it first as a control process using the six control elements discussed in Chapter Three. The Jewish model of creation, belonging to the first camp, for instance, is interesting if God is viewed as representing a control process.

God has:

1. the source of power,
2. the will that controls the power,
3. sensors that 'see,'
4. a comparator that says that "it is good,"
5. converters that convert the plan into reality, and
6. the plan.

The above discussion can then be compared with the view of the second camp represented largely by the scientific theory of the Big Bang creation. The Big Bang model of creation, however, lacks scientific detail as to how it came about. This suggests that Science did not wish to sound like the religious camps by introducing anything abstract. The model, however, is excellent in terms of proposing the terms of 1) basic Energy and 6) the data or the Law of the Universe.

This model assumes a concentrated source of pure Energy out of which everything is made which corresponds very nicely to the religious power of God. Science does not describe how the other four elements are involved in the creation process. These elements are hidden from the average reader who for instance does not understand the basic teaching of Einstein's relationship, $E=mc^2$, which states that matter is made out of Energy.

The equation is an excellent explanation of how God converted (5) his power (or his Energy) into matter. Science further separates itself from the religious model by ignoring the actuator or will (2) but obviously something did indeed actuate or trigger the Big Bang. The sensors (3) as well as the comparator (4) are included in the complex probability theory that essentially states that each atom or molecule contains an inner sense mechanism and tight controls that only allow certain things to happen.

The third camp accepts the common truth as to the origin of the universe having begun with Energy and Law. The third camp, however, requires different definitions that include a *why* as well as viewing creation as a continuous process. Creation is defined as creating a future reality that contains something new. In other words, creation is the controlling or changing of the future. Creation is a special type of change in which the direction of change is known, but the details of the final result of change are not necessarily known. Creation is typified with the unexpected additions of data occurring during the steps or time of change.

To further explore the third camp view, it is easier to start with your own daily experiences of creation. Consider for example, the simple desire or goal to create your own garden. Even though you begin with only a vague image of its final form, the goal of making the image real and manifest seems to drive you as you enter your yard and start digging or laying out the site of the garden. You may then go to a garden shop and browse and buy various plants or seeds for your garden. As these become planted you may again suddenly know that you need some rocks, and then perhaps a trellis followed by a surrounding hedge. Finally, after a month you are receiving praise for your beautiful "well-planned" garden. Each step toward the final creation consisted of the comparison of what was seen with the abstract starting image and then modifying what you were doing to satisfy the comparison.

You are well aware of the creative aspect of solving a problem that you have worked on for days, when suddenly a solution appears within your mind as you may be doing something completely unrelated such as taking a shower. At the moment of creation, the future is perceived as different than before and generally seen as being much broader in scope as well. Creation opens and extends the future.

As another example of a deeper inner creation, you may see a child trapped in a pile of lumber and then look for a way of releasing her. As you run toward the pile you suddenly have the image of the child being freed with one piece of wood being first removed. That piece of wood is seen as the key component toward the safe escape of the child. When you reach the pile, you twist that piece and remove it, and suddenly an opening appears that releases her. Later you find that you are unable to explain how you knew what to do without further endangering the child.

In order to continue to fully discuss and understand creation it is now necessary to define reality. There is an almost universal agreement that reality consists of two interactive pieces, the non-manifest and the manifest. In the modern world these two can be described as Law and Energy.

Law is the description of what is or is to be, while Energy includes the different forms of energy as well as the material stuff that comprises reality as described by $E=mc^2$. The ancients generally described Law as the masculine or sun principle and Energy as the feminine or moon principle. The Judaic/Christian religious view kept the masculine aspect calling it God, while the feminine principle became the Power of God or the Spirit.

To the ancients, both Law and Energy were the basic mystical elements and impossible to describe. They formed the beginning of a basic description of the universe and what was to be. Religions developed as means were sought to explain and control Law that was interpreted to be the source of the mystical and unexplainable occurrences.

Science developed almost in opposition to Religion. The early basis for science was that everything is tangible, understandable and measurable. The materialistic sciences, such as chemistry and physics, are called *hard sciences* because they deal strictly with measurable phenomena. The *soft sciences*, such as psychology and sociology, started with the acceptance of non-measurable or subjective data but have become increasingly more concerned with the materialistic approach. Science now generally agrees that if a phenomenon is not physical or measurable then it belongs to Religion and is not a part of Science.

It is not too difficult then to understand the angry outbursts and writings against Einstein (Callahan, 1931) by those scientists smart enough to understand that the very basis of science was threatened if science had to openly acknowledge and accept the mystical as a part of science. After Einstein pointed out the fundamental mystical consideration in science, other mystical models became commonplace (Capra, 1975). Others also pointed out that the very fundamental units of science, namely mass, length, time as well as energy, were also mystical and simple extrapolations of the old earth, air, water, and fire of the ancients (Bridgman, 1978).

Energy, however, is treated as being tangible and physical in most science textbooks, even though it is clearly proven that energy is only manifested as it changes its form such as in getting heat out of burning wood. No one knows what energy is, although its many manifestations are well known and studied. Energy still remains hidden and non-measurable when it is at rest and not changing into another form.

Law is also treated as being something other than mystical. Science speaks of discovering Law or of writing down Law, but it is seldom described in the same terms as Religion even though it is exactly the same. All experiences point to the fact that Law must exist before any physical change can occur to fully describe what can and cannot take place, otherwise there could be no cause and effect. Where is this Law? It, like energy, is only made evident when a change occurs. Both Religion and Science falsely equate Law to writings in their sacred books or technical journals. Law still remains a mystical element since it cannot be directly perceived or examined. Law is that element that describes what can and cannot take place. Law limits the size of atoms, defines the nature of forces, describes basic particles that can be made from energy, and describes an order that must be obeyed in the cosmos by energy and its manifestations such as described by the Evolutionists.

Law and Energy can be seen as forming the basic requirements for creation. A creation requires a description of what is to be as well as the energy to make it manifest. The third camp adds the method of how this process can be carried out in a practical world.

To understand creation as a common occurrence, it must be perceived as proceeding step by step with non-existent or infinitesimal time between steps, similar to the space between frames of a movie film. You may for instance be working on some problem and suddenly you perceive the answer in its completed form, or you attempt to convey an idea to someone when suddenly it happens. The normal materialistic viewpoint concerns itself with each frame and its description. Creativity requires bringing a power to the space between the steps or frames. Within this *no-time* space occurs the full description of the next step. This sudden description of what will be is called *gnosis* or instant data as initially described in Chapter Nine.

The world has long held various descriptions for the *gnostic* source of the knowledge that is required in the creative process. In general, the explanation is based upon an assumption that there is a subtle and hidden space that contains the complete unmanifested wisdom of all that was and will be. This space has been called by many names including heaven, the ether, spirit world or the world of the gods. One of the more recent discussions of this space called the *collective unconscious* was outlined by Carl Jung (1980). Whatever this source of knowledge may be called, it is referred to by many of the great creative people of the world as the source of their inspiration, ideas, or knowledge.

Access to this space, whatever or wherever it may be, requires energy. References have already been made to people who have to become psyched up or traumatized to do the supernormal or to find the wisdom to solve their problems. Many people have to be under the gun or have to face an immediate deadline before they can create. If a person is not filled with this special energy or fervor, then they proceed by the slow normal analytical method of comparing pieces of the problem with known data excerpts one by one until a close description or solution can be found.

Creation is not attained with physical or mental effort and trying to be creative is non-productive and even destructive. The creative person waits for the creative process or the steps leading to creation to happen after preparing the mind with the necessary attainment of words or models that will be required to describe the creation once it arrives. Creation requires quieting the mind, the faith that the insight will arrive, and then finding the source of a higher Energy that can power the creative process. Creation, in other words, requires the combining of Law and Energy as described in the original Creation.

If you wish to find creativity and to create a new world or reality, it is essential that you fully understand and increase the elements used in the control process as well as accessing the *gnostic* source of data or Law.

CHAPTER TWELVE
LIFE

It is important to first understand what Life means and what it entails if you are going to attempt to change your personal life. Life does not belong to the first Creation described in the last chapter but rather is added to it. Before Life appeared, the universe consisted of a process of the dispersion of Energy. Our planet was formed and gave up much of its heat and energy. Materials that would react together did so and gave up their individual energies, the outer layer of the earth cooled and solidified. The world was settling into equilibrium. But then Life suddenly appeared and was able to reverse this deadening loss of order and available energy called Entropy.

Two different forms of life appeared quite suddenly on the scene. One form could absorb the relatively feeble energy of the sun and use it to combine inert carbon dioxide, water, and minerals from the ground into a concentrated fuel or food. The other form of life consumed the fuel to become mobile and free to move about with capabilities for using the fuel to change the face of the world. In order to do both of these, Life had to create special molecules called enzymes to extract and concentrate energy for the stationary plant life as well as other enzymes to obtain energy from the fuel for the mobile animal form. The creation of the enzymes had to appear simultaneously with the two life forms.

The activity of the enzymes is controlled within both life forms by an inner control system with data that is contained within DNA molecules. This gives individuality and freedom to both life forms. For instance, plants can optimize their growth and then survive during the night without sun. Animals can eat and then move freely according to their inner data. Within both life forms exists an individual expression of Law or data to which can be added new Law if required. Higher life forms give evidence of their individuality with physical characteristics such as form, height, strength and mental capability differing from others within their own species. Variation in an individual characteristic such as the height of an oak tree follows what is called a normal distribution law[14] that is a further characteristic of higher life forms.

Most life forms are able to control their future to some extent. Some plants are able to project new growth into greater sun exposure or roots toward increased water supply. In general, life forms must control their future if they are to survive. This can be stated as: life forms that can adapt and change to future demands will survive, whereas those that cannot will probably die. In this endeavor, variations in each life form assist or hinder (Darwin, 1859).

Another interesting aspect of the higher and more complex life forms is that although they are highly individualistic, they must also exist in nearly perfect union with other life forms. Nature generally attempts to remain in balance and will quickly restore harmony by shifting some individual characteristics such as rate of procreation, dormancy, sociability, stamina, strength or endurance in the affected species. The slight shifting of individual characteristics over a large population and over an extended period of time results in large changes that are able to counter any imbalances.

This slight shifting of individual characteristics can also take place under intentional direction over a prolonged period of time (Schrödinger, 1992). A parent, for instance, keeps introducing new things to a child very slowly over a period of time without losing the union or relationship with the child. Similarly, political and religious viewpoints change very slowly without the majority of the people being aware of it. Any attempt to suddenly change anything is, however, met with

[14] See Chapter 2 pp.4-5.

resistance. As an example, it is not possible to suddenly change your viewpoint about a person or to change your taste in food.

The ancient Greeks had a very good description of life that can further add to the above discussion. Life[15] to them was evidenced by growth or puffing up[16] coupled with a very subtle exhalation[17] of something. As an example, unconscious persons can be tested for life by holding a smooth surface such as a mirror or a piece of glass up to their nostrils and observing if a fine condensation of moisture appears on the surface. This same phenomenon was also observed with plants. Growth and exhalation therefore characterized life. The Greek word for growth was *orgao* meaning "to swell and exude moisture," from which comes our word organic.

The power of some individuals to change their world was explained by the ancient Greeks as being due to the manner in which they breathed. Powerful people such as warriors, orators, people expressing strong emotions or exerting themselves had one characteristic in common. This characteristic was the manner in which they exhaled. Plants and weak individuals had a rhythmic, slow and gentle breath, but the powerful people had a very forceful and deep exhalation that came from their lower body instead of from their chest. The power was attributed to the forced breath just as life had been attributed to a gentle exhalation. This deep forceful breath, called *pneuma* in Greek or *spiritus* in Latin, became identified with the inner drive or power of an individual.

In the modern world, it seems strange to equate an individual's spirit to a particular breath, since the modern thinking would be that any breath follows or is caused by the brain's response to an outer situation. The thinking brain is considered to be in

[15] *zoe*, Greek
[16] *phuo*, Greek
[17] *psuche*, Greek

charge and controls the body, whereas the ancient model required the brain to respond to the breath or inner spirit. The controlling aspect of the spirit will be discussed in more detail in Chapter Twenty, but for now, it can be pointed out that the ancients' model may be far more accurate than the modern thinking. The power of the breath can be briefly introduced now with the simple reference to the times in which you encountered some new dynamic situation in which your first response was to gasp with a forced breath. Following this gasp, you many times felt that you were taken over by the situation and your brain and body responded in some uncontrolled manner.

The nature of breathing became important to our ancestors. India perhaps led the world in the development of a science of using the breath to invigorate the body and mind called *prana-yama* which means "control of the life force."[18]

The source of the higher power, evidenced by the forced power exhalation, was universally considered to be in the belly, bowels, or lower abdominal region. This region was considered to be the seat or heart of power, passion, and creativity in developed individuals. Even in the modern world you hear of individuals speaking of gut feelings, gut churning as well as inspiration rising from the guts. Further, the modern world associates the use of the breath as a method of calming the emotions by taking a deep breath, relaxing and letting the breath exhale slowly or by holding the breath. One interesting sign of leadership in a group can be observed by listening to the conversations. The leader will invariably speak with a lower pitched voice and with a more forced exhalation. Listen to someone, for instance, who is wishing to control or take command, his voice will lower in pitch with more exhalation. Ironically, almost everyone in the modern world has been conditioned starting at an early age to pull their tummy in,

[18] See Peck (1985) for *Elaboration on the Basics: Body Control*

tighten their anus, and to breathe in their upper chest, all of which prevent the full usage of the exhalation.

One very early definition of a human being indicated another aspect of an individual that has been lost through the centuries. The Greeks called humans *anthropos* that is derived from the word for an individual, *aner,*[19] and the word for looking at something with wonder or receptivity and openness, *optomal.*[20] The higher forms of a human were therefore able to fully see and were more than just physically resembling an individual *anthropoid.*[21] *Optomal* is more than observing, but is also associated with learning, being changed or being overwhelmed by that which is looked at[22]. The ability to see something clearly without your own bias or expectation is not, however, a common characteristic of the individual in the modern society who is conditioned to only see in part with a particular bias. As a simple example, it is very difficult for most people to see their family members or friends as they truly are. This is evidenced by the fact that they are seen as unchanging from day to day despite the fact that they are changing as much as the observer. The ancients found that special exercises or practices were necessary to see individuals and things as they truly are, such as being able to see an enemy as no different from your friend, to see your mother as no different from a woman on the street, or yourself as no different from a beggar or famous celebrity.

The above characteristic of looking with openness can be exemplified when you are attempting to impress some friends with a story about yourself. You watch their face very carefully to observe whether you are telling the story improperly and adjust your style of telling the story depending upon their

---

[19] *aner*, Greek: "a superior man"

[20] *optomal*, Greek: "seeing the Divine"–not normal vision (*blepo*)

[21] *anthropos* + *-oid*, Greek: "man" + "to resemble"

[22] See explanations of *dhyana* and *samadhi* in Peck (1998) Chapter 22: *The Practices*

observed facial expressions. This simple introduction into control can then be seen as looking, *optomal*, and changing the driving force, *pneuma*, to reach the desired goal.

The looking, the driving force and the goal are not normally easily perceived and, in fact, are generally hidden under the veneer of being civilized or of being controlled externally by your society. In general, what you see when you look is what you expect, desire or fear. The driving force of life is tightly suppressed by years of conforming to acceptable activity levels with surrounding people and interactions. The goal is generally already formulated tightly in your mind as to what you and the world should be. The ability to formulate new goals is also suppressed with a very limited and rigid image of yourself and world.

In order to change yourself and world and become more full of life, it is obvious that you must be able to fully *see*[23] a world as it is to become and then activate yourself in the new world to change it. The next chapter will discuss how the aspect of seeing can be changed by your view of the future or your goal.

---

[23] See Peck (1994) pp. 33-36 for Patanjali's teachings on "seeing."

CHAPTER THIRTEEN
THE FUTURE

Modern thinkers have a number of questions concerning the future. On the one hand, you know the inevitability of such things as death and taxes, yet you also know that people do shape or change their own future with strong willpower or dedication. The chief question is generally expressed as: Is the future all predestined or is there a free will in individuals that can shape their own future? This chapter attempts to convince you that you do have free will but that the exercising of your will must be continuous over a long period of time. Thus, each moment becomes an opening to, or a reflection of, your desired future.

As a simple starting illustration, consider a small tree in the woods that stands in the shade of the larger surrounding trees but has one lone branch that has grown well beyond all of the other branches in order to reach more sunlight. It is as if the tree put a great deal of energy into that one branch so that it could ultimately grow out for more sunlight. Obviously, the growth took a large period of time during which the tree continued to send extra energy and directions in the expectation of finding solar energy. The tree can be said to have directed and controlled its future with very small daily changes in cellular growth that extended some growth rates into the supernormal range while reducing others to a subnormal rate.

Humans are likewise able to add more energy into certain growth characteristics in order to reach some desired goal. They too can increase the energy into certain activities of the mind and body while decreasing the energy into other areas. This is commonly observed with the different scholastic paths in high school and college. For instance, compare the difference between the physical and mental output of energy and interests of students majoring in gymnastics from those majoring in physics.

Differences in mental and physical outputs are also evidenced in different actions such as performing some miraculous feat like saving someone's life as compared to doing the mundane activity of parking a car. The characteristics of an individual can change from approaching the supernormal to the subnormal.

Before continuing, consider two true stories about how the future was changed for two men as they reached for a goal.

I had a recent business meeting with a foreign black engineer working for a large American corporation when during lunch I became interested in his personal history. His story was quite inspirational as he told of being born in a primitive African farming community and then when hearing of the modern world resolved to seek that world and master it. He did!

I also had a close relationship with a Hungarian Jew who had spent his teenage years in a German concentration camp and was near death and starving when he was finally released and placed into a German hospital ward. One day, without family, friends or education, he suddenly told the other patients and staff in his ward that he was going to go to the United States and become a physicist. He recalled the ridicule from the men around him after that incredible pronouncement. It was only a few days later when he was found to have an advanced case of tuberculosis and of course everyone thought that was the end of his foolish dream. However, he recounted this story to me as we were fellow students studying physics in Colorado, USA.

These two stories are excellent examples of changing your own life. The final results in both stories are almost miraculous and unbelievable, similar to the one long branch of a tree reaching for sunlight. The explanation, however, cannot be limited to the miraculous final results but rather must focus upon the many small mystical steps that were taken to reach the final goals.

The change in both men took place over a long period of time with many separate steps. Each step, however, was like those of the tree, in a specific direction or toward a particular goal. Each step for the men required many different characteristics to be changed rather than just the rate of growth. As for instance, the changes in acquiring new language skills, social perception, opening to new sources of assistance, exercising faith and dedication, and the energy to change. Just as the tree was directing its inner changes toward reaching the sunlight, the two men were directing their inner energies toward reaching America. With a constant willful dedication of reaching America, they would be sensitive to English words, to references to America in newspapers, conversations or magazines. They would find statements that could lead to doors that might open to America and its culture. Their interests likewise would be directed toward subjects that belong to the future world.

Each step when viewed separately becomes understandable as for instance, seeing a magazine in English discarded in a trash heap and then salvaging it. Hearing of a course in English and enrolling in it. Attending a movie about technology in America and writing letters to institutions that offer more information that point toward the goal.

How does your willful dedication of reaching a desired future affect your inner control system? In the above cases, the increase in wisdom can be considered as a change in data resulting from the dedicated future. This change in data also exerts a force upon the other elements within the individual's control system resulting in variations of the ranges of the converters, sensors, comparator as well as the actuator. The individual with a goal or dedicated future can be described as living within a field of interaction that shapes the future similar to a tree in the field of shadow reaching for increased sunlight. Religions express the possession of a goal or dedication as freeing you from your bondage or ignorance and then opening you to the seeking of further freedom and enlightenment.

The presence of an ongoing goal can therefore slightly vary each element of your inner control system. The data describing your personal world changes such that more and more of the new world becomes real as each step reveals a new insight. The sensors change so as to become more sensitive to the anticipated. The converters shift within their limits as your entire body gradually shifts in posture, tensions, and expressions. The comparator becomes more sensitive to the attributes associated with the desired future. The actuator increases the flow of energy within your body to meet the increased demands and the excitement of a changing self in a changing world. The demand for energy shifts toward the more creative energy that can stimulate your mind to opening to and identifying a continually created new experience every day.

This inner change to create or find a new self and world can be explained in terms of the small variations of your individual traits taken over time which gives you a new character, personality and identity. These changes in your individual characteristics are normally well within their normal range requiring no supernormal changes such as discussed in Chapter One. As an example, consider the changes in your body if you decide to become friendly at a party when you were first feeling rejected, bored and in the midst of unfriendly people. Your facial muscles gradually change as your frown becomes a smile, your eyes open wider, your posture straightens, your shoulders pull back and your voice becomes deeper.

The discussion so far leads to the common experience that your expectations as well as your immediate world shape or control your individual control elements such that you may fit into that world with its expected interactions. The determining factor for changing is your mental perception of what will be or your expectation of your desired future. The inner muscles, organs, sensors, comparators and energy sources then change to manifest that reality. The changing of each control element is, however, generally not a conscious control but rather proceeds automatically according to the mental data describing the new desired future world.

Other examples of the power of an envisioned goal are common in the superhuman deeds personally experienced or reported in the news. Reporters seem to be attracted to stories in which a small woman does some impossible physical feat to save someone's life. There was a recent example where a local man became pinned under a large forty-foot tree in the woods. He cut the tree and as it fell it turned unexpectedly and landed upon him. His wife not only was able to lift the tree sufficiently to free him, but also then ran some distance for help, thereby saving his life.

The above example contains the formation or change of the future with a self-created image of what the future must become. The future is envisioned perhaps in many different ways and then one possibility is selected and then made quite real in the mind and then made real in the outer world. Such creative acts can be defined as the intentional changing of the future to conform to some initial mental image.[24]

The above wife, for instance, had an instant mental image of lifting the tree herself and then she made that image become real. She was obviously able to find supernormal strength as well as the supernormal ability to perceive a future in which her husband could be freed. There was no violation of Law, of

[24] See Peck (1999), Chapter 7: *Knowing and the Word.*

course. Some supernormal courage, strength and endurance was, however, quite obvious.

This chapter so far has introduced a tree's capability to change its own future with a directed growth and has described the stories of two men and their dramatic unfolding of their desired futures as well as a woman doing a supernormal feat. At this point you may be asking, "Is there accepted scientific evidence that your present willful intention or dedication can actually change your future?"

Interestingly, the answer is "Yes." This is based, in part, upon results of experiments that have been ongoing over ten years in the Princeton School of Engineering.[25] Their work can best be introduced by considering an interesting characteristic of machines noticed over the past few decades. Universally, all machines, both mechanical and electronic, have the annoying quality of not performing consistently from moment to moment.

For instance, machines tend to speed up or slow down due to small or unknown extraneous forces. This poses a problem when manufacturers want their machines to perform consistently. Even mechanical clocks vary due to small changes in temperature, air currents, and vibrations. (Even if a clock is put into a vacuum with nearly a constant temperature on a vibration free stand, it will still vary.) When scientists reached for more and more precise control of machines, they also found that the variations continued although the variations could only be detected by some very precise or sophisticated measurements. This time variation in performance of machines was called *noise* and each machine could be characterized with the range and magnitude of its noise.

Princeton's research can be described as discovering that an observer of a machine could affect the machine's noise or small

[25] For an excellent review of this work, see Jahn & Dunne (1989).

variations if the observer could continually focus on increasing or decreasing the operating speed of the machine.

The operators were not capable of grossly changing the operating speed of the machines such as stopping them or making them operate beyond their designed values. As for instance, if one of the better operators at Princeton were to concentrate continually upon a pendulum clock for a full day, with their full output of controlling energy, the actual time variation of the clock would be expected to be only about a minute.

To restate Princeton's conclusion in terms of this chapter, the present dedication or intention of an individual can change the future operations or characteristics of a machine within the machine's possible range of values. This machine variability can be compared to the variability of an individual that was discussed in Chapter One. Both the machine and the human can be expected to exhibit supernormal behavior as their characteristics vary toward the normal limits of operation. Princeton's conclusion could therefore be applied to a human attempting to throw a ball toward a target as discussed earlier. The ball thrower would be expected to find that on the average the ball would be closer to where it was desired to go with intention than without intention or expectation. However, a consistent hole-in-one game could not be obtained by a golfer nor continuous love matches by a tennis player.

Another important requirement that must be acknowledged regarding changing of the future is that the existing Law cannot be broken. It may be possible to change or add to Law as will be discussed shortly, but the basic prior laws of nature cannot be ignored. In other words, the men discussed above could not suddenly disappear and then reappear in America with all of the tools that they needed. Instead, they had to undergo a large number of steps to get there, and each step was according to

Law. Each step might require a supernormal effort, but it is nonetheless statistically possible.

The above discussion can be summarized as: the changing of the future requires a concentration of Energy that is equal to the final change obtained. This creative act cannot violate the existing Law but may add new Law. Changing your future is therefore only possible provided that:

1. The change takes place with a large number of small steps.
2. It is a creative and willful intentional act.
3. It does not violate Law, and
4. the correct energy is used to equal the change.

The final major requirement, that is hard to find and maintain, is the continuing existence of a dedication that serves to direct each step. The future should become the expression and fulfillment of your present dedication. When your desired future becomes your present dedication then the oncoming present becomes one of the many predestined steps toward that desired future. As an example, the possibility of a Hungarian Jewish boy who survived the Holocaust with little education, no family or friends and in poor health going to college in America becomes reality with a large number of dedicated individual steps.

This phenomenon can be stated that an individual has the chance to make a number of decisions at each step of his or her life. If each step is directed toward a particular direction or goal in the future, then the final steps may open to a very different world from the one that random or conditioned choices would have led to. This can be summarized by fully elaborating upon the first question of the chapter such that without a dedicated future, your future is predestined, but if you have a strong continuous dedication then your free will actuates the future to allow its manifesting.

What happens without a dedication? At any particular moment without the control of a dedicated future, you are completely subject to your conditioning that includes your desires as well as the interpretation of the demands of the outer world. Your resulting activities become essentially robotic or described as being in a rut as your body and mind follows your inner programming.

With or without a dedication, each possible world that you can find varies from the others in many very small ways. As for instance, the difference between your world on a good day and a bad day consists of many very small changes. With dedication, a number of sequential choices are made, each with a definite direction in mind over a large number of steps. This will result in a very different future than what would have been obtained with the normally random or conditioned small choices.

Another important question arises. Is there any limitation as to the amount of change that can be made to your dedicated future? For instance, can you create a world that includes things not presently known or accepted, or can you go beyond what is the present Law? In order to answer these questions, the definition of Law as described in Chapters One and Eleven must be recalled. Law was defined as being the governing rule of the universe which controls what was, is, and will be. With this definition, the next question becomes, "Can Law be added to or is it rigid and complete in itself?" If Law is unchanging, then the future must also be fixed; however, if the Law can be added to then the future becomes undefined in the present. Since the future does appear to be changeable as already argued with the introduction of Life, then the assumption will be that additional Laws can be added to the universe. Another manner of expressing this concept is that if the future is to be changed then new concepts and Laws must be added to the old Law.

If Law can be added to, then experience indicates that the old Law cannot be counteracted or negated, but rather that added Laws conform and are built upon the old Law. In other words, a Law cannot be created that will nullify or change any of the Laws that it is built upon. One indication of this idea is that if you could take back a simple transistor radio that fits our modern Law to some time period before the creation of the transistor, there would not be any scientist or laboratory that could begin to explain the radio. The Law of that time did not allow even the possible construction of a transistor. At that time, the transistor radio would have been considered to be in direct opposition to Law and its operation would have been described by most scientists as being based upon some sleight of hand or fraudulent scheme.

The ability to add to Law seems supported by the above discussion, yet many individuals within the scientific as well as the religious communities reject this concept. These people think of reality as being fixed and unchanging and therefore must have been unchanging since either the 'Big Bang' or the seven-day creation of God. This belief makes true individuality impossible since all aspects of Life are already written into the old Law and must therefore be preordained.

Some modern arguments for an unchanging Law are built upon the increased understanding of the organization of DNA and the knowledge that its organization determines most of the basic characteristics of an individual. Materialists are therefore very eager to use this information to indicate that individuals are preordained and predestined by their DNA. There can be little doubt that it is perhaps true for the majority of the people for the majority of the time, yet the individual who does create a new world or Law becomes the expression of true individuality.

The next step in describing the attaining of a desired future world is difficult to understand in our materialistic society. This step can be described as, once a future is specified and dedicated to, the desired future now determines what will happen in the present unfolding moment such that the future can and will take place.

It is relatively easy to accept that your expectations of your future are shaped by your present activities, but how can your dedicated future also in turn determine what you are doing in the present? Some reverse connection of your future to your present is required. One way of thinking about this is to consider a common wives' tale that caterpillars will grow a heavy coat if a cold winter is expected.

To further emphasize the reverse connection of the future to the present, consider the Jewish boy described above finding that he had tuberculosis after he made his dedication to reach America. Instead of destroying his dream, it became instrumental in the fulfilling of his dream. It was as if his desired future imposed this illness in the present so that the tuberculosis would become the means of reaching America. The diagnosis of tuberculosis led to his being accepted for treatment at a charitable Jewish tuberculosis hospital in the United States. This charitable institution also became an instrument of his future that opened other doors that he required in order to obtain his dedicated future.

The future is open and not closed, and its power over the present can be confirmed by unexplainable singular experiences commonly found in your life. For instance, many people experience how they encounter some unexpected bit of information that seems trivial but which becomes very important later. Examples are common of the life stories of people who had a strong dedication in their life to reach some goal. They generally all relate how some seemingly chance encounter, some unusual decision or occurrence later opened up doors that would allow them to continue to advance toward their goal. Although at the time many of these experiences were seen as catastrophic, in hindsight they are generally described as very positive and certainly related to their goal. In retrospect, the steps are experienced as having been guided by the chosen future or by a higher power.

Probably everyone has experienced that feeling of some activity being foreordained or where you are taken over or possessed. It may be the sudden outburst of emotion in some group, or the sudden offering of advice, or the sudden act of saving someone's life. Invariably, the results are perfect in furthering some basic dedication or concern. A common expression is given by many people that they do not have the slightest idea as to how they will obtain some goal, but they know that they will—and they do! Their future goal, and not necessarily their conscious thoughts, determines what actions will take place in certain unfolding moments toward that goal.

The difference between having your past controlling your present or your future controlling your present is manifested in the unfolding or oncoming moment. The chief difference is whether you are critical of your world or accepting and enjoying it. The controlling influence of the past and its conditioning is most often experienced when you are doing unchallenging routine and repetitive work. At these times, the sense of time and awareness of external events may be lost such as experienced in driving long distances. The past is evidenced with the learned skills and concept of the self that keep the vehicle on the road and the rising complaints about the distance, noise, traffic, etc. The future controlling the present is always experienced as an external force that essentially makes you do something without a conscious choice as for instance when you speak out in a group or advise someone without prior planning. This force is, of course, dependent upon your dedication or goal and can allow you to either evolve or regress. Your free will is therefore only expressed in the moment of defining your future or your way while the Divine or some higher power directs the steps.[26]

These creative intentional acts can best be described in the words of a short ancient document that speaks of these steps,[27] "Whatever is desired and made a dedication to, becomes reality. The power of knowing all is not reached for but rather abides within."[28]

The modern Westerner steeped in materialism and cause and effect has difficulty in accepting that futures are individualistic and may be created by the individual in the present. The average Westerner has a belief in the future, and that belief determines the acceptable perceived reality. This belief however, is generally only maintained by the consensus of society or its institutions and consequently, this dependency upon society suppresses individuality. There is a method, however, of joining futures between individuals that strengthens the mutual future over that of an individual. In other words, if you can find someone else that can share your dedication, then your path to that future can be enhanced.

One basic axiom that is often quoted is that if a husband and wife face a common challenge, they become tightly joined in meeting the common task. One of the greatest motivators for bringing people together is to present that group with a threat. The early histories of developing religions demonstrate that persecution can become a strong force in solidifying and starting the expansion of a church or group.

In comparison to the above, consider that much of modern marriage and family counseling is generally directed first to the defining of problems and then finding some cause of the prob-

[26] Proverbs 16:9
[27] *krama*, Sanskrit
[28] See the *Paratrimshika*, verse 29, in Peck (1998).

lem or someone or something to blame. Many times, the result is to identify the clients or patients as victims who are unable to change themselves. The resulting therapy is then oriented toward minimizing conflicts in daily life and interactions by essentially accepting themselves and their world as unchanging, non-threatening, and passive. The relationship therefore becomes at best a static relationship.

The above static relationship can be compared to 'first love' when a couple finds a relationship that includes a common future that seems to beckon them both. In reaching for this common future, they find that they are in almost perfect agreement as to their present thoughts, feelings and actions. As they let their future unfold, they find more and more union and bliss. However, the reaching for the future is lost when the people around them tell them that their future cannot last and that their bliss will disappear. The couple then start to attempt to "prove" to others and themselves that they have a common future and therefore respond to the moment instead of their dedicated future. They then worry about whether what they say or do is correct and how it will be interpreted. Their data is now the same as that used by average couples locked in a static relationship. Once this is done, they rapidly fall into the normal relationship of conforming to the outer world without a common dedication.

It is important to recognize three basic types of individuals and their futures. There are those who cling tightly to maintaining their present world such as with the first love couple above attempting prove or save their relationship. There are those who attempt to improve their world exemplified by the start of the first love relationship. Then there is the vast majority who wishes to bury themselves or to sink into security and withdraw from the challenges of life.

You are familiar with all three types of individuals. The first type envisions themselves as much younger than they are. Their future world is seen as a continuation of their past. Their past, present and future world is unchanging. They typically complain about the changes in their present world. They reminisce old times as they get old and then look forward to entering heaven which is essentially a repeat of their old life, experiences and acquaintances.

The second type is constantly looking for more. They look for new acquaintances, experiences, thoughts and deeper relationships with their present friends and loved ones. They are looking for a better world and work toward that goal. Their future lives are seen as evolutionary or as going beyond their present capabilities and experiences, and interestingly their anticipated future goes beyond their inevitable physical death.

The third type of individual and future is easily seen in perhaps the majority of middle-aged people who give up their aspirations and instead look for security. They look forward to retirement and isolation from the troubles of the world. These people speak of dying and going to their eternal rest or of sinking into oblivion.

This chapter can be summarized as saying that your future is changed by having a mental image of your desired future coupled with the faith that it will occur. It is manifested in each moment leading toward that future. This manifesting of your future then requires the generation of the proper energy to equal the amount of change that must take place. If the change requires more energy and external support than can be generated or found at once, then the change takes place in a series of steps. Each step must be within the limits of capability of the individual and the external world.

BOOK THREE

CHANGING

CHAPTER FOURTEEN
INTRODUCTION

The last Section concluded with the teaching that your future is determined by your dedication which can be manifested generally only by a number of steps. Each step is normally limited because of the lack of any extended control capability. This section offers techniques for expediting and increasing the magnitude of each step.

Changing yourself and your world must start with an inner mental or conative change. A controlled change must be preceded with an image or data of the desired end result. That image must be consistent with the world or role that accompanies that change. Simply trying to physically correct or control some characteristic generally fails. Your conditioning tells you to try harder, your experience demonstrates the folly of this approach, yet you were not taught another method.

Almost everyone has experienced how simply wishing to change does not work. Changing yourself and your world is accomplished by using a systematic and scientific method. The early chapters described the basic control system followed by chapters describing each of the six elements of the body that are used in controlling. The following chapters will instruct you as to how these single elements can be altered singly or in unison to control your whole world.

Each of the following chapters discuss one control element and the changes that result from changing that element. It should be recognized, however, that you may be required to change more than one element to effectuate some desired result.

CHAPTER FIFTEEN
CHANGING YOUR DATA

To change your data is to change what you are or might be to what you will become. To change your data is to evolve—or regress.

One of the first problems is to understand the difference between adding new wisdom versus changing your inner controlling conditioned data. For instance, reading about what you want to be is not the same as becoming what you want to be. At best you can add temporary data that can be used to play a new role with, but a great deal of repetition of that temporary data is required before it becomes permanent as discussed in Chapter Nine.

A fundamental assumption in changing your data is that each world, role or mood that you might be in has its own set of complete data. Within each world, everything fits together so that all of the data is consistent. If the pieces of data of your world do not fit together, then your world becomes uncertain and unreal with no solidity. Sometimes a mental shock can, at least momentarily, create conflicting data resulting in confusion even as to your own identity. Therefore, if you wish to change any part of your life or some particular data, you must change your entire world to fully fit that small change in data. This requirement is the reason that individuals are generally unable to change any single habit or attribute since that change does not fit with the existing whole person. They are afraid or reluctant to change their whole self and rather assume that they can pick and choose various attributes to put on or take off. This wholeness of your data is illustrated when you see someone attempt to put on a smile to cover up their anger. Their failure to look happy with only a forced smile becomes very apparent to you. You have also experienced how anger can be overcome, by letting go of it, shaking it off and then fully stepping into a new role with its complete unique data.

The history of people changing roles or what or who they are probably started with the putting on of a fixed mask. Primitives are known to have changed themselves by putting on a mask, paint or tattoos and then becoming the force that they represented. It continues today with your clothing. You may dress up and when you do, you become someone much different than when you put on your old work clothes. Similarly, you are not 'yourself' until you have combed your hair and done your usual grooming. The clergy, policemen, physicians, teachers all know the importance of the uniform or clothes as well as the proper facial expression. You cannot be a physician to a stranger if you are giggling with your tongue hanging out, you must be somber with a strong concern showing on your intelligent and kindly face.

Putting on a somber, concerned, intelligent and kindly face is done daily by many people, yet how is this done? Generally, the answer is that they first mimicked someone else or became like someone else that they knew about. It may have been a teacher, parent, movie star, or even someone they heard or read about. Even though they may have originally practiced in front of a mirror looking intelligent or somber, it was not enough to just look like someone else. They had to actually become intelligent and somber. Because clothes or a uniform was not enough, they had to find a force behind the clothes that was strong enough to change their data as to who and what they were.

To become someone else or to find the inner force of someone else is relatively easy and starts in childhood. Parents are many times startled to find their child mimicking them in their games such as when a young girl will address her doll in exactly the same tone as her mother would address her. Children likewise will 'become' their heroes in imaginary games in that they reflect the force of that hero as coming from within themselves.

You are aware of how you start to assimilate the mannerisms and expressions of others with simple associations with them. You will start to have the same facial features, as for instance if they frown, you also start to frown. If they happen to stutter in their speech, you also find the pressure to stutter. If they tell a sad story, your countenance also takes on a sad nature.

Children in growing up are forced into accepting a fixed and limited image of themselves that they learn to accept as forming the basic data as to who or what they are. This limited image comes primarily from the parents who find difficulty in seeing their child with capabilities much different from their own. Children are therefore inculcated with a family image of who and what they are. This complete set of conditioned data is almost impossible to overcome later as an adult except with a strong dedication and effort to take on another role.

Religions have claimed to be able to offer new data to their members such that their world can be changed. Some ancient religions, for instance, had a plethora of gods with each god being a unique person with unique powers and personality. (These gods may be perceived as having been the forerunners of today's stage and screen characters.) These gods were then used for examples or sources of data as to what a person might become. No doubt, children were continually compared to these gods and then told that they should become like a particular god. That god then became a model for the child to first mimic and then by continuing this for many days the model became permanent data as the child gradually took on the desired characteristics. Modern children are also taught to mimic some ancestors, godparents or other chosen models of their parents such that they become indoctrinated with permanent data.

Some of the very early-recorded worship techniques cite how the adult worshipers would call forth some god and then have that god change them by entering within them and overpowering them.[29] That process thereupon gave the worshippers the power of that god that was integrated within their conditioned self and data. As an example, a warrior could call forth the presence of a warrior god who already had the warrior characteristics fully integrated into his data. By assimilating the fully developed data system, the change could be quite quickly obtained and made permanent with constant usage. Another example is when you mimic some other person. As you mimic that person you take on his or her general characteristics which includes the particular desired characteristic. However, you cannot take on only one of the characteristics.

Modern religious worship on the other hand, generally requires a separation of the worshippers and their god such that the worshippers must ask for particular characteristics to be added to their existing selves. As for example, many worshippers pray to a god to ask for some attribute such as love, bravery, wisdom or fortune rather than expecting to become that god. Unlike the ancients, modern worshippers, for the most part, do not seem at all anxious to become significantly different and certainly do not wish to become god-like, but rather only desire to possess an added single attribute.

One major obstacle to changing your data or role is that you have been conditioned from childhood that you cannot or dare not change yourself. This starts in childhood when you are constantly told to be yourself and are severely admonished when you attempt to be like some other real or imaginary child. Your parents were very exacting in giving you data about what and who you were as well as deep fear and guilt in even considering changing that data. This conditioning is so intense that

[29] See Peck (1999), Chapter 9: *The World and Reality*

the majority of adults many years later cannot accept the idea that they can or do play different roles. One strong evidence of this is the distrust of actors. Actors can, of course, play almost any role and so they cannot be trusted to 'be themselves' and this raises all of the doubts, fears and guilt that you were raised with about yourself. This deep conditioning results in the peculiar situation that you have to be yourself no matter what you are feeling or doing or that every role is the same and you certainly cannot play different roles. You may for instance be deeply depressed, but if one of your friends asks if you are depressed you tend to answer in the negative since your basic conditioned image of yourself is that you are not one of those depressed types.

The early Judaic/Christian concept of sin is a good model for what keeps you from being able to change your data. Sin is an energy barrier that is handed down from generation to generation starting with Adam. This sin prohibits you from seeing the light or Truth and binds you to the world of mammon. It is evidenced by children who grow up with their parents' view of the world including religious and political beliefs as well as personal behavior characteristics. Almost all religions (and many institutions) teach for instance, that it is sinful to accept the data furnished by another religion (or institution). What this interpretation really means is that it is sinful to be open to other viewpoints and hence not open to further change.

However, many people truly attempt to find the inner self and to evolve into something new during much of their life. Children, for instance, love to be transformed as evidenced in their imaginary games as they quickly become something other than what their parents are subjecting them to become. As you grow older, this desire to evolve into something new is subverted as you 'take on the adult world' and become a 'pillar of the community.' This becoming a good citizen is of course fundamental in evolution and is a recognized necessary step in all religions.

However, the next steps in spiritual evolution then require the building upon the already learned social responses of the mind and body along with the earlier desires as a child. In other words, the childhood desire to evolve into something new is continued once you have learned to conform and have mastered the social world.[30]

The original writings of religion, in contrast to today's society, discuss transformations such as being reborn and taking on a new body, finding a greater light and understanding, finding increased strength and power over others, becoming a sage and changing the world around you. The religious transformations can be compared to some modern philosophers who speak of becoming a superior person, as for instance, Abraham Maslow, who describes the unusual characteristics of the "self-actualizing" person[31] that corresponds with Nietzsche's *ubermensche* or "overman."

There is a necessary special output of energy required in order to find and use data that goes beyond the conditioned and social data. This power is within each individual and corresponds to that of an enzyme that overcomes a barrier potential and allows energy exchanges to take place that normally would not do so. The barrier that you experience prior to a significant change is certainly an energy barrier potential. After the change, you have more energy and creativity than before, so the change does in fact release more energy than what is required for the change. This barrier potential energy must, however, be overcome and surprisingly it is actually relatively simple to do, but very hard in terms of conditioned data. The technique is to let the inner power rise and act as an enzyme to start the change without any opposition. This stage is often described as surrendering to your

---

[30] Ibid. Chapter 10: *Changing your Reality*

[31] See Goble (1970) pp. 24-35 for a description of the "self-actualized."

goal, sacrificing the self for a greater self, being reborn or finding a higher self.

The first question that needs to be faced in changing your inner data is very simple, "What do you want to become or be?"

The second question is, "Are you willing to expend the required energy to make the change?"

The answer to overcoming your reluctance to change is to first concentrate upon becoming a person seeking change. This process was alluded to earlier when it was stated that you could choose your direction of travel into the future, but the Divine controls the steps. Children are capable of putting this concept into practice even if they do not understand what it means. If they could not do this, they would be unable to fit into the image of what their parents want them to be. They could not be good as expected or study hard to get good grades. They see Life as a process of becoming or of beginning with each day. Children are a good example of the striking verse of the Gospel of Thomas that states, "Seek always to begin and never know death."[32] Seeking should only be applied to the new and unexpected, although most people use seeking to prove what they already know or the rightness of what they are. The child's world is readily seen in their imaginary games where they must first enter the game with some role to play and then trust the game for its unfolding or what steps are to be taken into the unknown. People who work with children know the power of getting children to envisage a challenge as a game and to become something more than what they are.

How do you therefore set up the data for a direction that you wish to go? You typically first find the role that is suitable for starting the trip. Can you remember as a child setting yourself up to play a common imaginary game of being some type of an

---

[32] Robinson (1988) Verse 18

explorer? You probably spent a number of minutes at the beginning of the game discussing what you had to have or should take with you. In discussing this you also started to take on the role for the trip such as starting to feel resolute, brave, determined, alert, etc. By the time the preparations of the trip were decided upon, all of the children had their respective roles tightly in place.

Although most adults would probably deny that they play roles as do children, if they think of being with their parents, children, boss, the clergy or some visiting dignitary, they might identify these times as playing roles. You put on a role when you speak to a sales clerk or someone that is supposed to serve you versus the role you play to give help to someone else. Both of these roles are already present as data and all that is required is to choose the data that fits the required role.

The data for the role that you desire to play is generally obtained from someone else who has already been where you are wanting to go. This started in school, when as a child, you listened to a teacher and later to a professor, coach or mentor. This data is also obtained by example or subtle suggestion such as when children grasp the idea of what their parents want them to be with minimal prompting. In fact, some children are quick to develop and do much of this on their own volition because they are able to foresee what role they are supposed to take on. They thereby convert their view of the future into immediate data that they then use in reaching for the required role.

Because not all children are able to take on an expected future role suggests that some special talent is required. Perhaps the talent hardest to acquire is the talent of being able to work hard to obtain your desires. Maslow argued that almost everyone has sufficient imagination, yet very few have the energy or will to reach for their future and make it real. This is related to the old adage that most people bypass opportunity because it looks like hard work.

When it becomes necessary in your life to find a special type of data that can be described as the creative answer to an immediate or future problem, then it becomes essential that you learn to access the *gnostic* or an intuitive source of data. This requires the ability to search through many feelings, subtle concepts, imaginations and images. As an example, creative people all tell how they have only one good idea out of a hundred or so ideas. They also describe something within themselves that can be explained as the action of a strong comparator that allows them to forget the ninety-nine bad ideas and keep looking for the one in a hundred good ideas. During this search a strong dedication assists in allowing the one good idea to shine forth as discussed in Chapters One and Eleven. Creative people can therefore be characterized as being open to both their own as well as others' thoughts yet using their very active comparator to reject the many bad or unrelated thoughts. The faith in finding *gnosis* is essential as well as the ability to quiet your own mind to the unwanted random data as you seek for some specific data.

There is another trick in finding data that starts with some idea or desire that you wish to contemplate. Consider, for example, that you are wondering if it would be a good idea to change your religion. Normally you think about the possibility in terms of acceptance by others and then drop the idea. The better method is to fully create a mental story and see yourself becoming a member of the contemplated religion. It then should be made real in your mind allowing you to mentally live that role over a period of time sufficient to give you the experience of actually living the religion. Certainly, you must go beyond the imagined shock or admiration of others and experience the daily changes in your life. Then you can accept or reject the data associated with the envisioned change. Similarly, you may consider changing your job, again make the change real in your mind such that you include perhaps living in another place, new friends, a different daily routine, etc. Fully playing this inner mental game can invoke the data arising from *gnosis* as data appears that you would have never considered before.

In conclusion, perhaps the easiest method to change or to learn how to change your data is to follow that method used by children in creating new roles to play. Similarly, the data source or *gnosis* leading to creativity is obtained by becoming a seeker for truth without bias or expectation, but with a strong dedication and faith of that which is sought.

CHAPTER SIXTEEN
CHANGING THE CONVERTERS

There are two major types of consciously controlled converters operating in the body, the muscles and certain functions of the brain. Both of these require similar techniques for increasing their performances. This chapter will start with the muscles since they are more readily apparent and better understood. The discussion of the conversion processes in the brain will follow.

There is a general feeling that you cannot change your muscles other than by exercising or working out over a long period of time. Although this is mainly true, you can also change how your muscles respond by assuming different roles. As an example, if you decide to play the role of a strong person, there is a shifting in tension in your muscles that can be quite noticeable. Your posture changes typically with your shoulders moving forward, your legs become separate and slightly bent, your arms and legs seem prepared to lift a weight or do heavy work. If you then imagine that you are lifting a heavy weight, you can actually feel work being done and with sufficient imagination, you can quickly tire yourself out. This can be explained as the subtle working of muscles against muscles such as extensors against contractors. For instance, one set of arm muscles attempts to extend your arms while the opposing muscles pull your arms in.

People who are used to lifting weights know the importance of preparing the body for lifting by some such preparatory mental imagination. There is also the use of the proper attire to help establish the role such as athletic shorts and sweat shirts that can assist in preparing the mind and hence the body for exertion.

Similarly, if you are about to undertake some fine or delicate movements, there is also a change in role. You shift your muscles into being sensitive and responsive with typically a gentle flutter of the fingers to loosen the muscles. The preceding preparation for lifting a weight would leave you almost incapable of doing any fine mechanical adjustment with your fingers.

In general, your converters are changed by envisioning the future activity that is going to be required of them and the role that fits that activity. Your expected future requirements change the actuator. Another way of saying this is that you must not attempt to be the same conditioned person or role in all activities if you are to optimize your actions.

The stretches or *asanas* of yoga are excellent preparation for increasing the performance of the converter muscles. When a mental or imaginary stretch is done first as suggested above, the muscles are envisioned as control elements rather than simple extensors or retractors. The muscles can become precision control elements capable of being positioned exactly where they are required. In general, the old muscle exercises of the East are done slowly with a tight connection to the controlling mind or data. This can be contrasted with the average Western exercise that rapidly moves the muscles to and fro with no attempt to control the muscles in-between their extreme limits and with no direct concept of the future usage of the muscles.

Additional control of your converters is obtained by adding additional data or by increasing complex motions. Again, the East uses many exercises that require balance or interaction of a number of muscles such as in standing upon one leg and then moving the other leg. A simple introductory exercise is found by walking very slowly such that the body moves in very slow motion. The legs must be lifted and slowly moved forward or backward just as if it was being done in normal walking. This simple exercise also reveals how little the conscious mind is knowledgeable of the basic motions as evidenced when you are not sure whether your arm moves forward and back with a particular slow leg motion.

Modern society considers public stretching as poor manners even though it is very beneficial. It is interesting to note how few people will stretch after sitting over an hour in an auditorium. One can learn to stretch without the outreaching of the arms with a bit of practice by using the contractor muscles against the extensor muscles mentioned above. Giving your muscles more attention and controlled motion will result in their better response when required.

The changing of the brain converters follows the same basic rules as for the muscles in that they need preparation and the introduction of a good model or the role the brain is to play. The brain converters are, however, probably less exercised than the muscles in the majority of people. This lack of exercise is evidenced in attempting to read some difficult text if you normally do not read. You may remember back to your school days when you could have easily read and comprehended such texts. The old adage that you cannot teach an old dog new tricks applies very well to the aging population of the Western world who have allowed their minds to go unexercised and unchallenged.

The conscious brain has several functions including remembering data, imagining and producing temporary data, analyzing or comparing data from the interior of the mind and body to the outside world. All of these functions can be called conversions either of feelings, sensory input or analysis into new data. To develop and exercise these converters, they must be given problems requiring the same type of functions.

One of the reasons that the mental converters are not exercised is due to the modern desire to be entertained. Entertainment relies upon some external data to substitute for using the inner data, actuator and converters.

Perhaps the best way to develop the converters of the brain is to entertain instead of being entertained. This approach requires you to invent and play a role. This is, of course, the opposite of the desires of the majority. When you fully play a role with some dedication, you will use all of the functions of the brain, and if you attempt to increase the role and the game, you will start to develop the converters of the brain. In increasing the intensity of the role, you add more excitement and fervor or energy. The conversion of what your sensors perceive of your outer world becomes more efficient and active as you interact more and more with the world. In reaching for your dedicated future, your brain converters must touch the future found in the subconscious or the creative spaces. This exercise is, of course, the advice to fully live your life if you wish to evolve.

If you find yourself committed to duties that prevent you from playing with others, you can still attempt to convert the doing of the duty into a game. As for instance, if you are watering your lawn, you can become the world's best waterer, carefully applying the optimum amount of water onto the lawn and garden. To the duty can also be added other functions of the brain such as watching your neighbors and creating an imaginary game wherein you are a secret agent observing some nefarious actions that you have to uncover.

You may also find yourself digging deeper into some mental pursuit such as attempting to understand someone else's behavior. This type of exercise can be watched while the goal is being pursued, noting each step of the process. If this type of mental exercise is perceived as being similar to physical exercise, you can find the ability to control your converters much the same as you do in heavy or delicate physical labor.

Yet another exercise is to ask questions of the inner and subtle brain functions such as, "What is really happening when I get upset or emotional?" Again, in pursuing the answer to this question, the various functions of the brain can be observed, controlled and strengthened.

One conversion process hidden deeply in the brain, converts *gnosis* or intuition into mental words and images. It is exercised primarily by using your imagination, curiosity and willingness to explore. For instance, contemplating your own death is a common start, but even thinking of doing this presents some basic obstacles that discourages most people from pursuing this type of approach.

The converters in the brain are therefore developed by reaching deeper and deeper into the creative space of the mind or opening more to the subtle feelings and images of the brain rather than the conditioned memory banks that require little conversion. This can be summarized as using the brain to seek answers to questions that constantly require explanations beyond what is currently known or found.

CHAPTER SEVENTEEN
CHANGING THE COMPARATOR

Perhaps one of the control elements that is easiest to vary is the comparator. The function of the comparator is to compare what is being experienced or thought of with stored or temporary data. In general, how well the comparator works is related to how much attention you pay to what you are doing or how 'fussy' or particular you might be.

The activity of the comparator is almost directly proportional to the opening or activity of the actuator. By simply increasing the energy or fervor that you apply to some activity, your comparator also becomes more active and sensitive. As for instance, if you are tired and bored while cleaning your floors, it is very easy to miss spots and not clean every section. If, however, you are cleaning for some purpose and place an energy or fervor in what you are doing, then you can become meticulous as the comparator is quick to point out each dirty spot.

Most of the time, your comparator becomes less responsive with routine actions and habituation, particularly if you start to minimize your effort in doing some repetitious action. This is the result of having little energy due to your reduced activity of your actuator. Changing the data such that a task is constantly viewed as being new and exciting can therefore increase the sensitivity of the comparator. In general, the data should include a necessity for a higher performance or quality level. This is exemplified for instance, by perceiving your efforts as being highly important when your role is being a government inspector attempting to prevent some deadly threat from eliminating society. Another method of increasing the activity of the comparator is to imagine that you are really on your deathbed and you have been granted a special gift of being able to relive some part of your life. In such a case, of course, even your most objectionable tasks could be viewed as wonderful.

Modern society tells you that you must 'try' and everything will be fine. In this case, however, the typical result is that the response of the comparator is set too far. That this is so is evidenced by the results as you attempt to control some situation or activity. In general, as you try harder, you become more judgmental and critical forcing the comparator to reject at a higher and higher level of sensitivity. Fault can be found where only a small deviation from the desired result would be normally found. As for example, you may desire to wash your car. You may then see the task as very important and you will attempt to get it "perfect," Your comparator then works overtime as it notices the dirt in-between the license plate and the mounting and then the rim of dirt around the edge of the hubcap. With such a comparator, you will indeed take hours as you try for perfection. An overactive comparator is also noticeable in trying to teach your own child as compared with helping someone else's child. The tendency is to be hypercritical of your own child while more accepting of another child.

The proper functioning of your comparator requires sufficient and proper energy, so be sure that you do have the proper energy. If it is comparing subtle data with temporary, converted or conditioned mental data, then a higher form of energy is required. This is evidenced when you have an impression or feeling of what some statement might mean, but you cannot fully 'grasp' or 'interpret' it. After a few moments of 'struggling' you tend to feel a weakening and fatigue that can be as real as the loss of energy in doing heavy physical work. This process takes a great deal of energy and in many cases, time. When you do not have sufficient higher energy, you find that you quickly fatigue during the attempt and perhaps accept some lesser interpretation that you know is not fully correct or may even be false. This accepting some lesser interpretation is known as poor thinking and can be directly related to the reduced sensitivity of the comparator.

Setting the proper level of the comparator is done primarily through the desire and faith in the outcome of reaching for goals. For instance, if you are confident that you will construct a sturdy wall with rocks, your comparator is set to a high level and each rock placement must be just so. If, however, you have little faith in the outcome, your comparator may approve a simple stacking or a mound of rocks as being sufficient.

Happiness and evolution in life can be directly attributed to having your comparator set to a proper level such that a union without judgement or concern can be obtained in all that is done.

CHAPTER EIGHTEEN
CHANGING YOUR SENSORS

You are seldom aware of your sensors, since in general, their activity is determined by the situation that you find yourself in. As an example, if you are looking for your lost keys, your vision is increased. Similarly, your hearing is quite active if you are concerned about what a child might be doing out of your sight. The roles that you play set the level at which your sense organs operate and the intensity of the play sets the level of your actuator.

This suggests that the first major step of changing your sensor organs is to change your role and actuator. Instead of being only an employee, imagine that you are from an alien planet sent to observe the characteristics of Earthlings. Become a critic of what others are wearing in terms of the expression of individuality. Notice how individuals use different facial expressions in speaking. Add the role of being an observer to whatever your present role might be or increase your curiosity of what is going on in your surrounding world. Instead of becoming caught in a rut, seek to keep finding more experiences even if it only starts with studying the motion of one of your fingers in some repetitive task.

Other examples of increasing your senses involve the stimulation of fear such as a fear that some feeling in your body is the precursor of some possible fatal disease. Another is the fear that your house is being broken into or that others around you are gossiping about you. Fear, of course, increases the attentiveness and interest of something in the outside world that can be deliberately used. For instance, some supervisors warn their employees of what might happen if they fail to fully meet some routine assignment. Similarly, parents will threaten a child with punishment if they fail to behave in order to increase their sensory awareness and attentiveness.

The senses are largely controlled by intent. If your intention is to remain cool and calm, your senses will generally cooperate. Similarly, if you wish to be active and alert, your senses will likewise become more active. If you think you are dying of a heart attack, your senses increase and you can start to feel every variation in the heart beginning with subtle discomforts and leading to possible pains in the chest. When you intend to perceive more, the senses become more active and aware. Similarly, boredom and inattention can reduce the senses. It is easy, for example, to become non-responsive to repetitive noise such as outside traffic sounds or music from a radio. However, when a new sound is added, such as a woman screaming or child crying, your sensors suddenly become sensitive and fully respond.

Since the senses are generally dulled with accustomed sounds, they can be resensitized with some forms of meditation[33] such as concentrating upon an inner sound that is called the *nadam* in India and tinnitus in the West. Tinnitus is generally considered to be an illness or at least some malfunction of the body, however, in some Eastern schools it is considered to be related to an inner creative energy. You have perhaps noted the ringing in your ears during a fever or severe illness or after some trauma. One explanation for this is that it is the sound of higher forms of your physical energy flowing to heal, develop or maintain your body. Another point of interest is that most prepubescent children report hearing the *nadam* almost constantly. This may be associated with the higher energy associated with their rapid growth. Unfortunately, it is apparent that most adults learn to ignore their *nadam* as they mature, possibly as the result of reducing the sensitivity of their sensors. Thus, your *nadam* becomes less apparent with the reduction in

[33] See Peck (1976) Chapters 6 & 7

the intensity of the inner flowing higher energy as you seek your old comforts and security.

To find the *nadam*,[34] one procedure is to search the inner quiet for the sound (called 'the sound of silence' in some groups) and then let that inner ringing *nadam* blend with the sensory inputs from the outer world. The results are quite unexpected since the inner sound can become relatively so loud that you cannot believe that anything on the outside can be heard, yet subtle sounds and sensations are perceived.

Meditation can be used in attempting to thoroughly open to and perceive another person. This form of meditation requires the letting go of any preconceived notions of that person and directing your full concentration upon that person. The actuator must increase the inner energy such that the other person then becomes a powerful person exerting a powerful influence upon you. This state is called *samadhi* where you become subject to a chosen subject of your meditation.

The senses can also be increased through a complete relaxation of the body such as found in meditations that reduce the metabolism rate to approach a state similar to sleep, but with the continued awareness of the body and senses. This state may be the same as used by early hunters while waiting beside a game trail without motion, but fully alert. Marijuana is reported as increasing a similar sensitivity of the sense organs, but at the expense of being able to fully use the actuator and comparator or able to maintain a dedication.

Another technique that works to change the sense organs is using expectation. If you expect to hear or sense more, the sense organs respond to your expectations. If you are desirous of fully interacting with the world, your senses are sharpened as you find interactions with more and more things in your world. This

---

[34] See Peck (1994) *Yoga Defined,* verses 27-29 for discussion of the *nadam.*

is related to setting your actuator to supply more energy to the object that you wish to perceive. The chapter on controlling the actuator will discuss this further.

CHAPTER NINETEEN
CHANGING THE ACTUATOR

Changing the actuator or will is generally a major problem. The problem can be approached by considering the factors that are known to reduce or turn off the actuator or will.

It has already been mentioned that your willpower fades as you view a lengthy arduous task with little perceived reward at the end. Many people report having a problem of even getting out of bed in the morning since they feel that only drudgery and pain awaits them. Lack of will can start with unsatisfied counter desires or fears and doubts.

Depression is one medical term for a lack of will and is generally diagnosed at two levels of either neurotic depression (mild) or psychotic depression (severe). The people who experience periods of excessive will as well as periods of lack of will are labeled as bimodal manic-depressives.

Depression is associated with changes in the body chemistry, indicating that the interrelationship of the mind and body is a problem. The body normally produces natural stimulants for both the mind and the body and these are diminished with depression. Medical treatment essentially replaces the normally produced stimulants with a sedative and a biochemical actuator that maintains a basic level of energy flow to the body and mind. However, this induced energy control is outside of the normal mind control system and can produce robotic-like reactions in many treated people. In other words, medicine replaces your personal actuator or will with a chemical substitute that cannot be altered by the patient and hence you lose your individualistic control.

This leads to the question of considering again what is an individual? Much of the modern world denies the spiritual aspect of life and evaluates an individual by means of physical and mental responses that do not require creativity, insight, or originality. The individual is judged strictly by how well the body and brain have been conditioned to perform societal requirements. To this philosophy, the will of the individual has little meaning.

This judgement of individuals is also evidenced in the opposite state of depression that is called mania. Mania, to the modern society, is having the actuator set too high. Treatment of mania is similar to that of depression as the individual's actuator or will is replaced with a chemical that suppresses the will. However, one problem exists to the modern researcher in this field, and that is that mania is associated with the great people of society. Many of the individual creative innovators can be diagnosed as being manic. Maslow labeled creative people as being self-actualized or of having their own control over their actuators or will. It then becomes highly questionable if mania is good or bad. The best that can be said is that it depends upon the personal dedication that goes with the mania.

This leads us finally to the chapter topic of how can the actuator or will be modified consciously?

The first obvious step is to change the data concerning the description of the self and world which is discussed in Chapter Fifteen. The view of the outer world must be changed and replaced with a positive world that presents a desirable and attainable future. The actuator cannot be fully activated if a positive future cannot be perceived.

The next step is to increase the ability of the actuator to turn on more power; however, this requires a new learning process that is generally very frightening to most people. One way to achieve this is to find more intense, vivid, interactive and powerful relationships with others. This is exemplified by John Wesley, founder of the Methodist Church, who attempted to be fervent in all that he did. This may have been the lost 'method' of the

Methodists[35]. The early Hindus likewise taught that one should observe *tapas* which originally meant having fervor. (Both fervor and *tapas* are derived from the root meaning “fire”). The modern Eastern and Western worlds do not advocate fervor or tapas, but rather the opposite nature of being submissive and conforming. Fervor is, therefore, generally interpreted in these modern times as meaning religious adherence, as is *tapas*, and not as being actively alive and on fire.

You have, in general, two different and carefully controlled levels of power when interacting with other people. You have the lower level that is turned on with people that you do not particularly care for and a higher level for those people that you feel comfortable and safe with. You can see these two levels in operation, for example, when you are angry with a friend. When you interact with this friend, you become what might be called reserved and cold, or else you treat the friend as a stranger or someone that you are not particularly interested in. You can also experience when you are excited with a friend and yet you cannot put more energy into your actions because of some inner restraint that you can feel. For instance, you can say, “Here I am very excited, but somehow, I don’t seem to be able to feel excited!” You were conditioned at an early age to use these two levels. For example, you were limited in your energy output in the classroom where you had to comply with a classroom level of acceptable behavior and response. When you visited others with your parents, you were many times instructed to be a lady or gentleman and to control what you say and do since these people are strangers. This level was also taught as being respectful to others or of being modest. You were taught not to be fervent.

Similarly, you found a limited level of mental imagining. You were perhaps punished if your thoughts ‘got out of hand’ or you

[35] See Peck (1999) Chapter 4, last paragraph.

spoke up with some 'wild' statement. You were admonished to control your thoughts and to keep them under control. You were not to become too excited nor were you supposed to become too reticent. Not only were you required to control the level of your thinking, but you were also to control the level of your physical actions.

This past conditioning of your energy level is so strong, you fear that if you go beyond your conditioned limits something dreadful will happen. Generally, this is perceived as making an ass out of yourself, or of getting others mad at you. In terms of your own thoughts, the fear is that you will go crazy if you allow your mind to increase its pace. You may also be afraid that the mind will take over and that you will then do some horrible action.

"Do not get your expectations up!" or, "Don't get carried away!" These statements are very common and thoroughly conditioned into most people. It is similar to "Remember your place," or do not do anything that others in your family or social status would not do. You are taught to not believe in finding anything in life that those around you do not have. This type of conditioning becomes very fundamental in limiting the amount of power that is applied by the actuator or the will to any activity that you are engaged in.

"Just who do you think you are?" This statement is generally thrown at someone who is bringing more energy into their activities than is done by others. Interestingly, if you rebel and become angry at such statements, you find that your actuator increases. Anger at injustice or ignorance can become powerful stimulants for the actuator.

The method of increasing your will or actuator is to become fervent in all that you do with a well-defined dedication in life. This may be done sometimes by breaking the long-range goal up into manageable steps. If problems are encountered in trying to increase the activity of the actuator, then you perhaps need to change your immediate goal and data to that of someone seeking a goal with fervor.

CHAPTER TWENTY
FINDING THE INNER POWER FOR CHANGING

The first criteria in finding inner energy or power is to recognize that there are a number of different energies or powers that your morning super-charged breakfast cereal cannot directly supply. Physiology is now able to list many specialized biochemicals that are known to be the sole source of energy to particular organs and functions of the body that are not contained in your normal food intake but have to be manufactured by rather obscure and not fully understood processes.

The body is not like a warehouse that has all of its biochemicals ready on shelves. These chemicals must generally be produced upon demand. It is true that the biochemicals that supply the basic energy to run the body are present in the blood waiting to be used, but even here, as any athlete knows, there is a very limited amount of immediate available energy. It takes time for the body to manufacture energy for special demands and this manufacturing operation must precede the demand.

As an example of the special energies involved in changing, consider the times that you had to wrestle with some mental problem or read some technical book and couldn't begin to think properly. You may have even described it as being due to your brain being exhausted or without energy. Similarly, you may have had to get out of bed suddenly to do some very heavy work only to find that you could not exert yourself until your inner energy production caught up.

The data for the functioning or control of the body is written in chemicals and not in words. The conscious mind must stimulate the right organs to produce or secrete the right chemicals that can then tell other organs what to do. The secreting organs, however, do not respond to words either. They respond to the state of the converters and the comparators and their demands.

You have no doubt spent considerable time and effort in attempting to talk yourself into becoming energetic and found that it was impossible, you rather had to put the body and/or mind into some situation that stimulated the production of energy.

Consider the following joke.

It was a very dark moonless night and Jerry was late so he decided to across the old cemetery as a shortcut home. However, as he hurried on being guided only by the lights far ahead, he suddenly fell into a freshly dug gravesite and then, of course, attempted to get out. He first tried jumping, then tried digging with his fingers to create footholds. He tried finding roots to hang on to, but all failed. He then decided that he should make the best of it and wait until morning. He therefore settled against one of the corners and quickly fell asleep. Sometime later he heard a thud and a groan and woke to hear someone else frantically trying to get out at the other end of the grave. Thinking that it was a waste of time, since he had already tried everything, Jerry suddenly, in a very positive voice, spoke up out of the dark corner of the burial pit saying, "You can't get out!" But, the other trapped person, on hearing that unseen voice of doom, did!

The joke illustrates the force of chemical data released by emotions as opposed to the reasoning power and trials of the first man.

There is another source of energy found because of someone's need or because you must assume some role that requires an inner higher energy or power. You may have, for instance, woken in the morning feeling less than enthusiastic about the coming day and then received a phone call from your neighbors asking for immediate help. You may have then found yourself bailing water from their basement or some such labor without any feelings of weakness. Then you went to work feeling invigorated and without the fatigue that you might have expected.

In most groups to which you belong, you play some role that probably varies from group to group. In one group you may be a follower and supporter of others, while in another you might be the strong person or the intellectual leader. In all of these groups, if the group expects you to have power in your role, you find it. For instance, if you are a supporter, you may find yourself working until midnight to help get ready for some party the next day, or if you are the source of strength, you may find yourself moving heavy furniture that you might normally have found difficult. The expectations of those around you provide some stimulus for finding an inner energy to do the job. The women who perform some nearly impossible feats of strength to rescue others have already been mentioned. Each of these women are certainly stimulated by the need of someone else.

There is another source of a higher energy that can be found by essentially becoming someone else. Instead of finding some need that stimulates your inner energy, you can also take on a role that already has an available source of an inner flow of higher energy. As an example, you may be aware of the tremendous strength that some mentally disturbed people can exhibit. The police report the difficulty in controlling some average teenager who is high on some drug. The teenager may require a number of men working closely together to place him in special restraints in order to counter his strength. Similarly, there are war stories of some wounded and dying soldiers continuing to go against impossible odds to save their buddies before they died.

The ancients had a system for increasing inner energy that is related to the above examples that centered upon an individual becoming "possessed" by something else. Typically, a worshipper would take on the nature of some god or become possessed by a god. After possession, the worshipper would have the described powers of that god, as for instance being able to find supernormal strength or endurance. Other powers would be related to healing others or of knowing the future or the offering of counseling to the village or individuals. You have experienced the power of possession when you allow some rising emotions in a group of friends or some group to overpower you and you find yourself ready to join in whatever may be demanded of you. Such is the power also found in mobs, rallies or demonstrations.

There is a related aspect of being possessed and that is found when you are overpowered by laughing or crying. In both of these states, if the laughing or crying is extensive, there is a following sense of being cleansed and stimulated with a new or higher form of energy.

There is another state of being *self*-possessed that is fairly common. This state was introduced in Chapter Thirteen whereas a dedicated person creates a field about themselves that contains all that is necessary to attain their dedication. This state is seen in many historical figures who were driven by their inner belief to disseminate some truth or social change. These people were described as having fervor or zeal which is an inner fire or source of a higher energy. Similarly, you have, no doubt, also found this fervor or zeal within yourself at times when you have become "possessed" with some idea or goal.

Performing artists have also found a source of inner energy that can be used to project their roles, feelings, or emotions out to others that is preceded by psyching themselves up or feeling the pressures to excel as they face the audience. This is similar to the individual who has to prepare a creative report for some group and then finds that he has to wait until the last moment so that he is "under the gun" and then, and only then, can he be creative. Many people also report that they work best under pressure. The above examples describe the usage of some inner tensions or expectations to release an inner creative energy. These individuals will sometimes seemingly devise or place themselves in some demanding situation to find the inner power.

You may have used a similar technique when you had to face an arduous task. You may have used such terms as *bracing*, *preparing*, *steeling* or *pumping up* yourself. It is as if you have to supply the need or stimulation to do the job from within yourself rather than waiting for some outside demanding or controlling force as above. This ability to find your own inner stimulation for the inner power is of course essential for the self-actualizing person, the evolving individual or the *ubermensche*.

There are many references to this higher energy in ancient writings although most of them have been incorporated into religious dogma and the higher energy relegated to an external heaven or source. One excellent example of this is the Indian *Rig Veda* which had its origins around 2,000 BCE or even before. This voluminous collection of short hymns can be interpreted by some unbiased person unfamiliar with the Indian religions as being descriptions of the various powers that can be obtained when filled with a higher energy in the form of a liquid called *soma.*[36] The various gods can be seen as symbols of the various powers that are fed *soma* and it becomes evident that *soma* can have many different powers depending upon the particular need.

The subject of *soma* and its increase was described in later writings in India such as the *Haṭhayogapradīpikā*, written about the

[36] Ibid. Chapter 10: *Changing your Reality*

fourteenth century and popular with modern Yoga enthusiasts (but for different reasons). Both the *Rig Veda* and the *Haṭhayogapradīpikā* as well as many of the other Yoga writings center upon the lower abdomen and speak of stimulating that region with pounding, pressing, tightening, churning, heating and stimulation with a strong exhalation or withholding of the breath.

Ancient Chinese writings likewise point to the lower abdomen as the center of the higher energy commonly called *chi*. *Chi* is generally described as being increased with heat, breath, pressure or slow churning. The early writings of Christianity can be easily interpreted (by non-Christians) to point to an inner power called a spirit or ghost that can give supernormal powers to the individual who masters it.

The Greek and Roman physicians, as mentioned, were trained to raise an inner healing power called the *anima* or *élan vital* within their patients. These physicians believed that it was this inner power that caused healing to take place although what they did to increase the energy is largely considered to be nonsense, lost or destroyed.

The teachings of the *Hathayogapradipika* about an inner source of energy mentioned above can be found elsewhere, but it is important to realize that the modern society negates any value in the basic teachings of stimulating the lower abdomen. Instead, our modern culture teaches to keep your anus and sexual muscles tightened at all times (particularly in public). Breathe in the upper chest and never exhale strongly. Keep your tummy muscles tight and your buttocks tight and pulled in so that your body is perfectly straight up and down. Rely upon medicines and pills and be fearful of natural processes. All of these practices suppress the inner energy.

The above example of increasing the inner power can be summarized as:

1. Become responsive to the outer world with eagerness, faith and fervor.
2. Have a strong dedication and trust each step toward it.
3. Take on the nature of someone that you admire.
4. Allow yourself to be possessed either with your own enthusiasm or that of others.
5. Keep your body prepared to generate the higher power.

Once the control of your life and world has begun to be mastered, then doors are found to open to an even greater world with an even higher form of energy resulting in what is commonly called ecstasy.

Ecstasy results with the prolonged or continual surrendering to a higher power rather than the nearly instantaneous stepping into a new role. Children will do apparently extreme actions to find it. As an example, consider one of the childhood games of "Ring around the rosie, a pocket full of posies," and "All fall down!" This game was originally based upon dying from the Black Plague that was evidenced with rings forming around suppurative nodes (rosies) on the skin, with protective flowers (posies) in the pockets, and the culmination of the plague when everyone fell down dead. Children love games in which they are killed, must not move, or are put under some form of a spell that overpowers them. "London Bridge is Falling Down" is another favorite game that culminates in being caught when the bridge comes down. Being caught elicits squeals of joy from most young children.

Some adults seek the ecstasy of being continually overpowered as they find joy and then seek even more joy. Sexual encounters are an example of this type of surrender although it generally ceases with the attained knowledge of each other. Careers can be ecstatic if each step along the way is perceived as the result of trust and effort with more steps to come. A relationship with others becomes ecstatic when there are common goals that everyone is working for and you surrender your personal immediate desires or fears as they arise. In such relationships it is found that there is always more to attain and to surrender to and the relationships are finally recognized to continue long after this life, game or play ceases.

When you can recognize that there are powers which exist that can override your basic conditioning, conscious desires or fears, the next step is choose what you wish to do and then find the inner power in the abdomen to accomplish it. As mentioned above, ancient peoples chose gods or spirits, but the wise or enlightened individuals taught of letting your own goals or dedication in life overpower you. This has been expressed in many ways, but in general, it can be stated in the words of Jesus, "Seek and you shall find." (Matthew 7:7-8)

A fifteenth century philosopher, Giovanni Pico della Mirandola, also expressed this concept very nicely with his idea that the generous God, for the happiness of man, allows man to be whatever he chooses to be.[37]

---

[37] "Oh unsurpassed generosity of God the Father, Oh wondrous and unsurpassable felicity of man, to whom it is granted to have what he chooses, to be what he wills to be!" (Mirandola, 1956, p. 8)

APPENDIX
An Ancient Model of the Control System of the Body

Everyone has heard of and used the terms soul, spirit and self, although just what they mean may be very unclear. One likely origin of these terms is an ancient Indian school (*Tantrika*) that was studying the origin of special powers that were acquired by evolved people.

The Indians appeared to approach the physical body as an elaborately controlled robot with its inner controls existing behind the scenes. The early researchers assumed the existence of different control elements located at different places within the body whose functions can be compared quite accurately with modern control elements used in engineering. For instance, the early model assumed that there was a center that supplied the data for who and what the robot was to be or do, a center of judgement or comparison for how well the robot's muscles or interactive devices was doing compared to the data. There likewise was a center that could adjust the sensitivity of the sense organs so that they could be varied according to need. There was a center that controlled the flow of energy that was complete with an overload element to prevent too much energy flow. And there was a center that supplied the energy.

The Indians discovered that the elements varied in their material or abstract natures, similar to modern controls. For instance, the data or data banks in the modern world are quite abstract being stored perhaps in a memory chip that compares to the abstract concept of a pre-spiritual element within you. The element that compared the action of the robot to the data was a bit more tangible as a spirit level since it had to have connections to the abstract data as well as the very real actions of the robot. The control of the robot's sensors or connection to the outer world were next in tangibility at the soul level since they were controlled by the comparators and again connected to the outer physical world.

The robot then contained the remainder of the elements including the muscles or converters that converted the commands to action, the physical sensors and the controls for the energy flow into the robot.

The originators of this model described the functioning robot as having different levels of existence from the very abstract to the very mechanical and described these levels as sheaths (*Shariras* in Sanskrit). The Pre-Spirit sheath was the connection to the designer of the robot and carried the data as to what it was to do. The next sheath was called Spirit. The Spirit was the inner observer of the entire system and compared the designer's goals with what the robot actually did. The next sheath was called Soul and it controlled the sensitivity of the robot so that it could become supportive to others or also to operate from within its own data. The final sheath was called the Self and could operate almost independently of the inner sheaths, since it could use data acquired from the outer world and stored in its brain and likewise control the power to whatever it was doing subject to outer feedback.

The following Table 1 lists the simplified levels of the individual and the functions at each level.

Table 1 Levels and Functions of an Individual		
Levels		**Functions**
Pre-Spirit Who and what I am.	**DATA**	Self-awareness and Identification, Consciousness, DNA and *Samskaras*.
Spirit Who and what I want to be.	**DATA**	Capability, Wisdom, Passion, Intention, Feelings, Intellect, and Role Comparisons.
Soul The interaction to the world.	**COMPARATOR** and **SENSORS**	Brain Controls, Sensory Identification and Intensity.
Self The physical manifesting body and brain.	**ACTUATOR**	Gate of Vitality, Self-Protector.
	CONVERTERS	Senses, Interaction, Communication, Energy.
	SPIRITUAL (Sun)	Creativity

The ancients considered separate comparators were necessary for the main capabilities of the body. Therefore, the action of the robot to the outer world was judged according to basic characteristics that are listed above. For instance, individuals can be identified by their capabilities, feelings, and roles that they play which are internally monitored and watched. Similarly, the sense organs were known to be controlled by an inner process that could increase or decrease the sensitivity of the physical ears, eyes, nose etc. according to the need.

One critical control was the Actuator located between the chest and abdomen that controlled the upward flowing energy. This was envisioned as a gate (*payu*) with an associated safety center that protected the body from too much energy flow. This center could also be called the center of the will in today's vernacular. The center of energy can be compared with the very modern knowledge that energy is the building material for matter as well as change. In the ancient world this element was considered to be feminine represented by the moon.

A separate center was assumed for the connection to the masculine supernatural or creative powers of an individual that was the center for insight, basic *gnosis*, Law, or knowledge (as truth). This center was considered to be represented by the sun.

A slightly modified listing of the centers is given in Table 2. The original Sanskrit is given for each characteristic (*Tattvas* or thatness) as well as its assigned Sanskrit letter that was assumed to be related to the vibration within that center. The *Chakras* (centers) (as originally used) are given with a slight modification to get better agreement with the *Shariras* (sheaths) or levels of the Self. Table 2 also gives an English rendition of the Sanskrit terms and in some cases, an example or further clarification. For more information, the reader should refer to Peck (1998).

Table 2 – The Ancient Individual Control System

Table 2		**The Ancient Individual Control System**		
1	*a*	*Shiva*	Masculine force, Law, Potentiality, Sun	
2	*ha*	*Shakti*	Feminine force, Energy, Manifested, Moon	
PRE-SPIRIT		**DATA**	***Muladhara Chakra***	
3	*s'a*	*Saddashiva*	I am this	I consciousness
4	*sha*	*Ishvara*	This I am	Distinction
5	*sa*	*Shuddhavidya*	I am This	Definition
SPIRIT			***Svadishthana Chakra***	
6	*va*	*maya*	Limiting	This is That
7	*la*	*kala*	Agency	Capability
8	*ra*	*vidya*	Wisdom	Wisdom
9	*ya*	*raga*	To color	Passion Intensity
10	*ma*	*purusha*	Spiritual form	Intention
11	*bha*	*prakriti*	Created form	Feelings
12	*ba*	*buddhi*	Concepts	Intellect
SOUL		**COMPARATOR**	***Manipura Chakra***	

13	*pha*	*ahamkara*	Action of the self	Comparison
14	*pa*	*manas*	Physical mind	Mental comparison
SENSORS				
15	*na*	*shrota*	Ear	
16	*dha*	*tvacha*	Sense of touch	
17	*da*	*chaksu*	Eye	
18	*tha*	*rasana*	Taste organ	
19	*ta*	*ghrana*	Nose	
20	*n'a*	*vak*	Speech	
21	*dha*	*pani*	Hand	
22	*ga*	*pada*	Foot	
SELF		**ACTUATOR (Will)**	***Anahata Chakra***	
23	*tha*	*payu*	Guardian gate	
24	*ta*	*upastha*	Lower secure place	
CONVERTERS				
25	*n'a*	*shabda*	Word	
26	*jha*	*sparsha*	Touch	
27	*ja*	*rupa*	Form, color	
28	*cha*	*rasa*	Taste	

29	*ca*	*gandha*	Smell	
Interaction			***Vishuddha Chakra***	
30	*na*	*akasha*	Ether	Communicati on
31	*gha*	*vayu*	Air	Separation
Manifesting			***Ajna Chakra***	
32	*ga*	*agni*	Fire	Energy
33	*kha*	*jala*	Water	Time-change
34	*ka*	*prithivi*	Earth	Physical stuff
SPIRITUAL			***Sahasrara Chakra***	
35-50	**Sanskrit Vowels**		***Shiva* aspects**	
LAW and ENERGY **(Back to top of Table)**				

References

Becker, R. O. & Selden, G. (1985) *The body electric: Electromagnetism and the foundation of life.* New York, NY: Quill

Bridgman, P.W. (1978) *Dimensional analysis.* New Haven, CT: Yale University Press

Capra, F. (1975) *The tao of physics: An exploration of the parallels between modern physics and eastern mysticism.* Berkeley CA: Shambala

Darwin, C. (1859) On the origin of species. London, UK: John Murray

Goble, F. (1970) *The third force: The psychology of Abraham Maslow.* New York, NY: Grossman

Jahn, R. et al. (1997) Correlations of random binary sequences with pre-stated operator intention. *Journal of Scientific Exploration.* 11(3)

Jahn, R. & Dunne, B. (1989) *Margins of reality.* San Diego, CA: Harcourt Brace

Jung, C. (1980) *Archetypes and the collective unconscious.* Princeton, NJ: Princeton University Press

Robinson, J.M.(Ed.) (1988) The gospel of Thomas in *The Nag Hammadi library* pp. 126-138. (T.O. Lambdin, Trans.) San Francisco, CA: Harper and Row

Maslow, A. (1968) *Toward a psychology of being.* New York, NY: Van Nostrand

Maslow, A. (1993) *Further reaches of human nature*. New York, NY: Penguin Arcana

Peck, Robert L. (1976) *American meditation and beginning yoga.* Windham Center, CT: Personal Development Center

Peck, Robert L. (1985) *Handbook for goats.* Windham Center, CT: Personal Development Center

Peck, Robert L. (1988) *The stone of the philosophers.* Windham Center, CT: Personal Development Center

Peck, Robert L. (1994) *The philosophy of Patanjali.* Windham Center, CT: Personal Development Center

Peck, Robert L. (1998) *The golden triangle.* Lebanon, CT: Personal Development Center

Peck, Robert L. (1999) *Power for change.* Lebanon, CT: Personal Development Center

Schrödinger, E. (1992) *What is life?* Cambridge, UK: Cambridge University Press (Original work published 1944)

Peat, F.D. (1987) *Synchronicity: The bridge between mind and matter*. New York, NY: Bantam Books

Pico della Mirandola, G. (1956) *Oration on the dignity of man.* (A.R. Caponigri, Trans.) Chicago, IL: Henry Regnery Co. (Original work published 1496)

About the Author

Robert L. Peck is by profession a research scientist working in the field of thermodynamics, holding many patents related to energy and its conversion and is currently developing artificial membranes that mimic natural processes.

He had mystical experiences starting in early childhood that opened the awareness of a very creative world and the transmutability of the physical. 'Bob' served in the Army as a paramedic in the Pacific near the end of World War II and by chance meetings was introduced into some of the Eastern practices including Zen archery in Japan.

Bob started teaching meditation in industry in the early Seventies at no charge for those who could not afford to pay for Transcendental Meditation. His Westernized meditation became in demand in local churches, adult education classes, and other informal groups. Many of the students, after mastering meditation, desired to experience more of the strange sensations that they were finding within themselves and agreed to enter into experimental groups that would look deeply into the various religious and developmental practices from around the world.

These middle-aged and middle-class Americans proved to be very adept at mastering many of the old and diversified spiritual practices. Their findings separated the results from any religious overtures that were normally connected with the usage or translations of early descriptive documents. Bob then had to read the original documents in the original languages to find deeper meanings and practices. It was in struggling with some of the original documents that he finally understood that some of these documents were, in fact, scientific writings and could be treated as such.

Index

www.ingramcontent.com/pod-product-compliance
Lightning Source LLC
LaVergne TN
LVHW050648100826
845148LV00011B/2037
* 9 7 8 0 9 1 7 8 2 8 0 8 9 *